Who Has The Final Say?

Who Has The Final Say?

Fi Wilkinson

Acknowledgements

Foreword by **Susie Richardson**, *Deputy Governor of HMP Winchester*

Front cover designed by **Karl**, *inmate of HMP Winchester*

Contributions from:-

> **Steven Hunt** – *Brother*
>
> **Jan Hunt** – *Mum*
>
> **Rebekah Campion** – *Friend*
>
> **Catherine Cornish** – *Friend*
>
> **Pastor Julia Franklin** – *Friend & Pastor at Victory Gospel Church, Southampton*
>
> **Vi Donovan** – *Friend*
>
> **Josh** – *Friend*
>
> **Lloyd Dyke** – *Friend*
>
> **Bethan Cotterill** – *Friend & line manager*
>
> **Pastor Ron White** – *Friend & Founding Pastor of Victory Gospel Church, Southampton*
>
> **Dave Birchall** – *Fi's dad's best friend & Fi's friend too...*
>
> **Olly Sherwood (aka King Jims)** – *Friend*
>
> **Reverend Cliff McClelland** – *Friend & Chaplain, HMP Winchester*

Who Has The Final Say?

Foreword

Whilst studying for my Masters in Forensic Psychology and trying to establish what God was calling me to do, I started reading about God's redemption in the lives of 'hardened criminals'. I realised that there is so much we don't understand about how to help other humans transform their lives.

Although evidence showed that conventional interventions in prison, focusing on attitudes, thinking and behaviour, can *sometimes* moderate the frequency and severity of crime, they were unable to provide a stay-fixed solution and although aimed at reducing harm, were rarely ambitious enough to aim to help people turn their lives around.

This 'evidence' appeared to be in great contrast to the faith-based stories I was reading about outside the lecture hall. Case studies were demonstrating the hearts of hardened criminals being changed from the inside out with the very core of these people becoming fuelled by God's love, manifesting not just in them acting differently, but in them being born into a new and sometimes unrecognisable life to any who had previously known them; an unexplained miracle prompting questions in even the most cynical bystander. These stories didn't fit with my very traditional Anglican experience of Christianity, but they intrigued and inspired me none the less and were something I secretly hoped to witness at a distance in my working life ahead.

In my fifteen years working in the Prison Service I've always stayed close to the chaplaincy departments and some of the most exceptional people I've met have been chaplains or their volunteers. Chaplains, although usually Christian, have a really important role in ensuring all prisoners get access to a minister of their respective faith, and multi faith working is something that prisons do really well. Faith and the role of the coordinating chaplain is embedded at the highest level of management in prisons, with ministers often being members of the senior leadership team. They act as a moral compass in decision making, a support for prisoners in crises, the facilitator in rites of passages for prisoners and their families, part of the network to support prisoners with accommodation and mentoring on release and the confidential 'go to' for staff members of any faith or none when they need to speak to someone outside the chain of command. They often give managers hope on difficult days in an environment that can otherwise feel hopeless. But there is something else going on in the chaplaincy at HMP Winchester… and it feels bigger than the work of mortals…

Throughout my professional working life I continued to ask God where He wanted me to be and in the summer of 2018, I joined HMP Winchester as the Deputy Governor, starting the same day as the new Chaplain, David, and joined a week later by his assistant, Cliff –which all felt more like God's timing than a coincidence. As I began to get my feet under the table, I learned of the number of churches and faithful people praying for revival as well as offering practical help to support the wellbeing of our staff. And then I met Fi…

If you have ever been duped into believing that all Christians are simply well-intentioned, naïve, passive people who dress up in their best outfit for an hour for a service on Sunday… MEET FI!

I first met this formidable woman of God as she was rallying 'her boys' (convicted offenders) for the final session of the restorative justice program she tutors and coordinates in the prison called 'The Sycamore Tree'. Before even speaking to her, it was clear that she wears the armour of God and is equipped to face anything. You can literally see the Holy Spirit reflecting in her face and this spreads through her very presence in a room. To compliment Fi and give credit to her as a mortal for what is achieved through her, would be to undermine her obedience in serving the Lord and her conviction that all things are from Him and that the glory is all His. But the difference we see in some of 'her boys' during and on completion of the programs she tutors is a testimony to some well-tuned team work between God and her wonderful team who facilitate the course.

'I will give thanks and never stop singing of his love for me... I will not be stopped or silenced', these words of Fi's written down. She is a woman of faith who is bold and courageous. In the face of setbacks and challenges, of which she and her family have experienced many in their loyal service, she continues to do whatever God calls of her and shows God's reckless love to any human who God puts in her path.

To have stood at the concluding session of a Sycamore Tree course, to witness the forgiveness of victims who share their story with active criminals and to see some of these men share a heartfelt and authentic "sorry" along with efforts at restoration of their crime, is a more profound experience than anything I expected when asking what God had in store for me all those years ago. As prison staff and managers we have a responsibility to ensure we look after those committed by the courts with humanity and to help them lead law-abiding and useful lives in custody and after release; this is our very statement of purpose; but it is the work and obedience of the people like Fi, in delivering such divine purpose, that, in my experience, gives our work its meaning.

Thank you God for putting me in Fi's path (or her in mine?). Thank you that the hearts of the most hardened are not beyond your redemption and that you continue to put well-equipped people in the right places to help bring about new beginnings. Thank you for all the faithful Sycamore Tree volunteers and the amazing people that come and share of unbelievable forgiveness and hope for the futures of the most damaged and dangerous in our society. May there be more examples of lives saved and free of prison, breaking the cycle of crime for the generations to come.

Tell us Lord… Who has the final say?

Susie Richardson, Deputy Governor, HMP Winchester

Who Has The Final Say?

Tribute

I dedicate this book to the memory of my Dad, David Peter Hunt (12/09/1947 – 16/10/2013). I would not be the woman I am today if it was not for your faithful commitment to praying for me at 5am every morning. Despite often wishing you had been here with me through this season, I am grateful you were spared the experience of seeing your 'little girl' have to walk through this valley, although it has been an amazing adventure of faith. Mum assures me that, just as she is, you would have been very proud of the way I have fought the good fight of faith, stood on the promises of God, and come through triumphant.

I have a mansion prepared for me in glory with you, but it was never for now. My work here is not yet done. I am on assignment and have started to take full possession of all that is mine, through Jesus, just like you prophesied over me before you went home.

Till we meet again in glory, I am eternally grateful for the thirty-five years we had together. I love you so much and long to share the testimony with you; I can hear your high pitched laugh as I write and know you are rejoicing with me, amongst that great cloud of witnesses.

Fi

(This book is published on the seventh anniversary of you being called home.)

Who Has The Final Say?

Introduction

*Blessed is she who has believed that the Lord
would fulfil His promises to her.
(Luke 1 v 45)*

Another Thursday has rolled round; we always comment that the weeks come and go so fast. The normal routine kicks off. Pete has left for work, Beth is en route to college and Anna is at school.

Before starting my working day, I have my time of prayer, pretty much going through the motions, if I am honest, asking God to keep my family safe and asking Him to bless a few other people along the way. Then a quick glance at a daily reading:-

*But when you ask, you must believe and not
doubt, because the one who doubts is like a
wave of the sea, blown and tossed by the wind.
That person should not expect to receive
anything from the Lord. Such a person is
double-minded and unstable in all they do.
(James 1:6-8)*

The apostle James wrote that we must ask in faith with *no* doubting. However, we must not forget that we have an enemy of our souls who is ever ready to throw doubts and fears at us. This potentially leaves us exposed in a very dangerous position of sitting on the fence and wavering between two opinions. This posture may naturally seem wise and somewhat *'safe',* knowing that nothing is at stake; a place of neutrality, requiring no commitment and options can be left open *'just in case'*. I can imagine this position of being undecided must result in a horrible feeling of unsettledness and confusion, due to considering something you should not be, and hence grieving the Holy Spirit.

This time with the Lord on the morning of *'just another Thursday'* was to become very significant and a continual testimony to the grace of God; I testify to never wavering through the season ahead.

I am employed as a support worker for a charity, *'Step by Step'*, where we support vulnerable young people prone to homelessness. This particular morning, I am heading across town to pick up one of my young people (YP) with all her belongings to move her into yet *another* new home. The weather is dry which is always helpful for such an activity. My YP safely loads up the car with all her worldly goods, which is always a difficult thing to watch, especially being a mother. The one item remaining to join the collection is a large flat screen TV. We will require assistance if it is to remain in one piece with the car already full to capacity. I tell her I will *"find us a man!"* to which she seems bemused and replies *"How are you going to do that?"* I have seen a lad working a cement mixer down the road and tell her to give me a minute... I return with the *'only too happy to assist'* young man who carefully finishes loading up for us. *(*She is only slightly embarrassed at what I have just done!*)*

Mission accomplished. Front door locked and keys put through the letter box for our host. We hit the road again and arrive safely at our destination. Once unloaded, the necessary paperwork is completed, signatures acquired and my YP wants a lift to her boyfriend's property. So funny to move someone in and within an hour they head straight back out, leaving a host feeling maybe that the YP is not happy or wanting to be there. On the quiet, I assure my new host that all is well and that my YP is happy and *will* return to sleep at the property that night... as agreed.

Off we go again heading back towards town. A familiar route and yet this time a *very* different one. We breeze through the speed camera on the way to the city centre and hit the red light, sat in the right hand lane. The handbrake needs to go on and the gearstick needs sorting. However, at this point, my left hand starts to shake uncontrollably followed by my left leg. I am now completely unable to do anything to keep us both, and other road users, safe. I recall thinking, *'Is this a stroke?' "I think I need some help!"* At this point, my YP starts screaming, not knowing what to do. Somehow, having removed my glasses which I often wear for driving, I instruct her to use her phone and call an ambulance. Dribbling from the left hand side of my mouth, I manage to tell her the road name before losing consciousness.

~

The emergency services talked my *'hero'* through saving my life, as I was apparently struggling to breathe. This required a lot of bravery from a seventeen-year-old on what was already a very stressful day for her. Before dealing with me, she had pulled on the handbrake; the car having stalled and then launched forward. I am told she ran round to the driver side door, undid my seatbelt, then as instructed by the emergency services, lifted me from the car and laid me in the road (there was no pavement), placing me in the recovery position. Apparently a couple of other drivers or passers-by stopped to help and provide support whilst waiting for the ambulance to attend the scene.

I'm not sure how long after this, I came to and found myself strapped to a stretcher in an ambulance, trying desperately to pull myself upwards but being unable to do so, all strength gone down the left hand side of my body. Despite being strapped down tight, I knew something was wrong as my right hand side was completely normal. I was faced with a firm but fair female paramedic who kept asking me if I knew what day it was and similar. I recall a younger paramedic who was very reassuring and told me we were going to be blue lighted to Southampton General Hospital where they would take good care of me.

Before we set off, a police officer found Pete's contact details and called him at work, explaining that the paramedics believed that I had experienced a seizure at the wheel. Arrangements were then made for my car to be moved to safety on a residential street. Until then, the car was completely blocking a very busy stretch of road. Looking back, the queue must have been quite something. Never again will I moan about being stuck in traffic! Whilst the vehicles backed up further and further up the hill, so the battle intensified to save my life.

The officer handed me my phone to speak to Pete and I asked him to let my mum and brother know what had happened so they could get to prayer. I also asked Pete to arrange for Pastor Andrew[1] to attend the hospital to pray. Despite being in the physical predicament I was in, I sensed and knew in my spirit man, that this situation was demonic and consequently would be approached from this stance.

Author's note: Throughout this book I will be dealing with some subjects of a sensitive nature and appreciate this could cause upset. Please remember when reading, I am simply writing my story.

---

[1] Senior Pastor of Victory Gospel Church, Southampton

Palm Sunday 1978

My predicted birth date was 20th March, my mum's birthday, but I was born on 19th at 1:50am at Kings College Hospital, Camberwell (*Home of the TV series, 24 Hours in A&E*). It was Palm Sunday and British Summertime had arrived. An extremely proud first time dad returned home to Guernsey Grove, London SE24. He had walked all the way with a grateful heart rejoicing and praying in the Spirit We lived in Herne Hill until September 1978, when we moved a few miles to SE19. Spurgeon Road, Upper Norwood was the land on which the Baptist Preacher Charles Haddon Spurgeon's estate had stood and our home was towards the bottom of the steep hill on the right hand side. This road sat at the highest point of Norwood cushioned between West and South Norwood and offering a spectacular view across South London.

Whatever the season, the view from the back bedroom window was always special, with my dad's desk positioned neatly in the bay. When we had moved from Herne Hill to Norwood, my parents transported a walnut tree they had purchased years back from Dorset and this was now situated in the back left hand corner of the small but pretty grassed garden. My dad used to enjoy feeding the birds and would often be sat at his desk with the windows open, whistling to attract their response and being delighted as the *'song'* kept going between them. Stepping stones, shrubs, a trellis covered in beautiful roses and a water butt made this garden special with lots of happy childhood memories.

How Firm a Foundation

On an extremely hot Sunday, 4th June 1978, we travelled to an Assemblies of God church in Bexleyheath for my Dedication. Pastor John Foster and his wife made the journey from Leeds to take the service.

Pastor John was a very significant part of my parents' lives; not only had he baptised my dad back in the sixties, he had also led my grandmother, Rose (my mum's mum), to the Lord three weeks before she died, ten years earlier. Her last minute decision was made as she was suffering on her deathbed. My mum and dad had prayed for her to come to know Jesus but, as is often the case, it required someone outside of the immediate circle of family and friends to come in and speak truth. Rose responded to the mercy of Jesus and invited Him into her heart. Without Pastor John faithfully preaching the Gospel, her eternal destiny would have tragically been *very* different.

There is a heaven but there is also a hell. It is tragic that so many people just assume that because they have led a *'good life'*, *'never hurt anyone'*, *'always helped people'* and maybe even attended church, that they simply go to heaven when they die. This is not the case and the Word of God has a lot to say with regard to our eternal destiny. When my grandmother said *'Yes'* to Jesus, heaven rejoiced and the angels declared *'Another one safely home!'*

Back to Bexleyheath… my parents promised that day to bring *'this gift from God'*, up in the ways of the

Lord and they committed to honour the will and Word of God. They prayed, along with every other believer in attendance, that one day, I would come to trust Jesus Christ as my personal Saviour for the forgiveness of my sins. This was not something that happened automatically and I had *not* just become a Christian.

The song that my parents had chosen for this special day was going to turn out to be prophetic over my life:-

How firm a foundation, ye saints of the Lord,
Is laid for your faith in His excellent word!
What more can He say than to you He hath said—
To you who for refuge to Jesus have fled?

Fear not, I am with thee, oh, be not dismayed,
For I am thy God, and will still give thee aid;
I'll strengthen thee, help thee, and
cause thee to stand,
Upheld by My righteous, omnipotent hand.

When through the deep waters I call thee to go,
Thy rivers of grief shall not thee overflow;
For I will be with thee in trouble to bless,
And sanctify to thee thy deepest distress.

When through fiery trials thy pathway shall lie,
My grace, all-sufficient, shall be thy supply;
The flame shall not harm thee; I only design
Thy dross to consume and thy gold to refine.

The soul that on Jesus doth lean for repose,
I will not, I will not, desert to his foes;
That soul, though all hell should

9

endeavour to shake,
I'll never, no never, no never forsake.

As a toddler, I apparently used to sing the first verse in a very high voice, together with my dad.

In April 1980 my brother, Steven, arrived. We have always been great friends with a shared *unique* sense of humour and I seldom remember us arguing as we grew up.

Being the older sibling *and* a sister, I took full advantage of being the one in charge... One year, Steven received a toy ride-on car called *'Billy Bumper'* for his birthday. He also had a *'not so good'* red and yellow ride-on car with a broken seat. As is often the case, being the older sibling *and* a sister, I took full advantage of being the leader and the one in charge of *most*, if not *all* activities and games we played together.

One of our favourite pastimes was what became known as *'That Game Again'*. This was played in the garden every Saturday in the warmer months. Both Steven and I drove around, myself now having acquired full ownership of *'Billy'* and Steven having to make the best of his other broken ride-on vehicle. He never *seemed* to mind although secretly, he must have resented the fact that I had taken his birthday present.

South East London to Southampton

I attended Downsview Church Hall for '*playschool*', a ten minute walk from home. Then from 1982 through to 1989 I was at All Saints School – another short walk from our home.

When I was ten and Steven was eight, we heard a powerful word preached in Chatsworth Church, West Norwood. This resulted in us returning home and both asking my dad to pray for us to ask Jesus into our lives. What an honour for my dad to lead both his children to the Lord on the same day. I remember kneeling down with my dad and brother and praying together.

If the short walks to playschool and primary school were a blessing then the best was to come. The entrance to Westwood Girls School stood no more than twenty paces from our front door and I attended here for my secondary education. These were mostly happy years until my health started giving me trouble in 1994 – the year I was to sit my GCSEs. I started suffering from trapped nerves in my neck and arms, resulting in hospital investigations and regular trips to an osteopath. I would put my arm in the air and get it stuck so that it was sheer agony to get it back down. I recall being off school one day, bed bound due to the severity of the pain. I called for one of the elders of our church, Alasdair, to come and pray for me and I remember listening to a song at the same time, called '*Rise and Be Healed in the Name of Jesus*'. Immediately, I arose and walked free.

I studied A Levels in Law, Politics and History at Merton College, Morden alongside a GCSE Maths retake. These subjects were mainly chosen since they were areas my dad could help me with – by now it was obvious I was not academically minded. Even the college was partly selected due to my dad working in Sutton so that most days I could get a lift at least one way. Other days required a ride on the 249 bus to Streatham followed by the 118 to Morden.

For my eighteenth birthday, I met my dad on his lunch break and he took me ring shopping; I still have the receipt that he gave me to keep. A beautiful diamond and sapphire ring bought from H Samuel in Sutton High Street. I am not into jewellery but this ring is very special, it is the only piece of jewellery I own apart from my engagement and wedding rings.

Somehow, I scraped the necessary grades to enter Westminster University, London. However, after two *long*, *boring* weeks I realised that studying and further education was definitely not for me. I remember my parents being very gracious the day I returned home earlier than expected announcing to them that I had quit and would not be returning.

Over the next few years, I worked as a shop assistant in a department store, a receptionist for a firm of surveyors and solicitors and then as a legal secretary practising in both family law and personal injury.

Pete and I met at Lansdowne Church, and started dating in 2000. Pete then proposed in January 2001 after a surprise day trip to Paris. I remember calling everyone we knew at an unsociable hour and telling them the news.

September 8th 2001, was a glorious sunny day and we married at Lansdowne Church. The ceremony started an hour late due to terrible traffic on the road from Brighton where Pete's family lived. While we waited, my dad and I were driven round the block a few times. This included a drive through Dulwich Park when my dad found it amusing to ask our driver to pull over whilst he wound down his window and asked a pedestrian whether she knew where the church was... clearly she could see the car contained a bride and was desperately concerned that she was unable to help. As we drove off and he wound up the window he laughed hilariously.

Our honeymoon in Portugal was during the week during which 9/11 occurred – which made for an interesting return journey. We then spent a week in Dorset before officially setting up home together in West Norwood.

Some six months later, Pete was made redundant; he was eventually offered a position working on The Isle of Wight; a good opportunity to escape the rat race of living in the capital. So after seeking the Lord, we upped and moved to the South Coast and ended up living in Southampton, having decided we did not want to live on the Island.

Our first daughter Beth was born at home in June 2003. This homebirth had been planned and despite things not being as straight forward as we had hoped for, we praised God for a safe delivery.

Another home birth was planned for early November 2005. However, Anna hit the scene four and a half weeks early and so was born at the Princess Anne on 4th October.

A couple of years later, Pete moved to an employer on the mainland, simplifying his commute and making things somewhat easier. Once both Beth and Anna were in school, I started work as a teaching assistant.

I struggled with severe back and neck issues for around eight years and had to trust all this time for a breakthrough. The devil fought hard but I testify to being set free. These years were very tough as anyone who has experienced long term issues with their head or neck will agree: relentless, draining and wearing.

From August 2016 to July 2017 we had a young man, Josh, who had been street homeless come to live with us. This was to give him a chance to sort his life out whilst having a roof over his head and lots of in-house love and support.

I note from my testimony book in August 2016, I wrote:-

Pete texted me to say:-

'Prayed for you today as God led, that as you go into strongholds of the enemy you carry the fragrance of Jesus and the roar of The Lion of Judah. You are a mountain lion raiding the heights of the enemy's stronghold in the pattern that your master has laid out for you.'

In January 2018, we took in a second young man under very different circumstances. After a year, he moved on, having thanked us for helping him become the person he was today.

We still see both of these young men and I count it a privilege to have been there for them both through difficult times in their lives and will remain supporting and loving them both.

I then started working for '*Step By Step*' April 2019, where I remain by the grace of God.

Boot Camp

*And we know that in all things God works for
the good of those who love him, who have
been called according to his purpose.
(Romans 8 v 28)*

A lot of what I have written down over recent years
has helped me to write this book as whenever God
moves I make sure keep a record in order to recount
his many blessings.

Whose Report Do You Believe?

Back in 2006, when Anna was six months old, out of
the blue I was hit with a severe case of irritable bowel
syndrome (IBS). This condition is extremely
debilitating and managing this whilst bottle feeding
and entertaining a toddler was something of a
challenge.

My parents came down to visit for Beth's third
birthday on Sunday 18th June and my dad prayed for
me. I was instantly healed and praised God. The next
day we enjoyed a wonderful family time together at
the zoo. Sunday through to Wednesday, I
experienced no symptoms and had no doubt been
touched by the Hand of God. However, watch where
I am heading with this one... On Thursday morning I
remember calling my dad while he was at work, very
distressed as the '*symptoms*' had returned. I thank
God for a dad who knew His God. I remember him
being completely unmoved by what I was telling him
and me trying to reason with him, telling him *"But*

the evidence is literally before me!" I remember him asking me *"Whose report do you believe?"*

I had a choice to make. I could choose to believe the '*symptoms*', this was clearly the easier option and required no faith. Or I could believe the report of the Lord whose report said I was healed. I chose to stand on the Word of God and I testify that from that day forward, I have never experienced any symptom. The devil is a liar.

Beth's Miracle

When I collected Beth from school on Monday 25th January 2010 she appeared clutching her head and complaining of a bad headache. We kept a check on her and carried on with normal activities, dosing her up with Calpol. After a couple of nights, and the headache having left, Beth complained that she could not see anything out of a quarter of her left eye. That Thursday morning, after dropping Anna off at pre-school, Beth and I saw a doctor who confirmed a significant loss of sight. He was concerned at this, given that the headache had gone. I was advised to take her to school whilst he made an urgent referral to the eye unit at the hospital.

Later that morning, having received a call to say the eye casualty were expecting us, I went in peace to collect Beth. She was sat in the school office with her winter coat, hat and scarf on, waiting for me whilst reading a book. I signed her out and we made our way to the hospital. After numerous tests they could not find any obvious cause for loss of sight and so we would have to wait six weeks to see a consultant and have a CT scan. We returned home after a draining day and the McDonalds was a welcome treat. From Friday morning normal routine continued with Beth at school.

Meanwhile, my mum requested that her church in London pray for a miracle. (These were the days before I attended Victory Gospel church.) Pastor Dennis took the matter *very* seriously and announced to the congregation that my mum had requested prayer for her six year old granddaughter.

Monday after school meant it was time for swimming lessons and on the way there, Beth announced:- *"Mummy, I can completely see!"* We returned to the GP and shared our testimony – all hospital appointments were cancelled. Glory to God.

Higher Ground

From April 2012, Tuesday nights at 8pm became a regular slot for meeting with my dear sisters, Faith and Elaine for a *'proper prayer meeting'*. Back then, I was a stickler for getting to bed *'on time'* at 9:30pm, knowing I needed sufficient sleep as I would want to get up to pray and read my bible. My sisters were more used to being up late and one of them lived on location. I would often be on edge that the prayer meetings would go on late (which they did!) and this would be worse on weeks when, due to reasons outside of her control, Elaine would arrive late pushing the meeting *even* later. Some weeks, I would have a set time in my head that regardless of what was going on in our time together, I would creep out the room, and get out the door and into the car. We could have been climbing to the top of a mountain in warfare and still I would head home.

In these powerful meetings we interceded together in the Spirit, engaging in warfare on behalf of others or in regard to situations we were facing between us.

I recall Faith saying to me very early on from when we first started meeting that I was a *'light leader'*, going ahead of others to mine for coal and gold.

What a Legacy

Most of us have had one of *those* phone calls at an unexpected hour; when you just *know* something is wrong. Wednesday 16th October 2013; I had just made breakfast when Pete asked me to come upstairs and sit down. He went on to explain that my mum had just phoned him to say she had found my dad dead in bed.

Shock hit immediately and I remember saying to Pete *"No, he's not dead..."* He had not been ill or shown any signs of being so, so of course he was not dead...He had only just celebrated his 67th birthday. Reality hit and, after I had phoned work, I packed a bag for a short stay and drove myself up to London to be with my mum and brother.

When you get to the bottom of Spurgeon Road, just before the familiar red post box, if you look to the left, you can see the back bedroom window, the bay where the desk sits. When Beth and Anna were younger, this was always a point of great excitement for them, knowing Grandma and Grandad's house was just around the corner. My dad would always appear as soon as he saw our car pull up and help unload our vast amounts of luggage required for a stay. I remember doing what we always did at this point and looked up but noted, unsurprisingly, the curtains were pulled across. As I turned into Spurgeon Road, I recall being cross when outside my family home, sat a private ambulance; the police having already been and gone. I rushed up the path and was agitated to be greeted by a man in gloves, opening the door and asking whether I was family... Surely, I should have been the one opening the door to a stranger; after all, this was *my* home. The timing of my arrival was such that I narrowly avoided the sight of my dad being carried out of the property in a body bag. The man did at least ask whether I wanted to see him before he left for good, but I chose not to, wanting to remember him with his beautiful smile.

Prior to my arrival, my brother had called Pastor Dennis from the church my mum attended in West Norwood. He had just that morning met for prayer and was then set to drive up to a prayer meeting at the Houses of Parliament. However, upon entering his car, he felt prompted within his spirit, to sit there and wait.

Within a very short time, he received the call from Steven to explain what had happened; the reason for waiting now evident. He was then able to be with my mum at the necessary time.

Preparations were made and, on Wednesday 30th October 2013, there was a service of committal at Norwood crematorium. The coffin was carried by Steven, my dad's two brothers, Mike and Alan, Pete, my dad's best friend, Dave and cousin Jem. Following the coffin was most surreal but the mercy and faithfulness of God followed hard behind.

A service of thanksgiving was then held at St John's Church, Thornton Heath. After Steven, Pete and Lottie (Steven's wife) and I had all stood and paid tribute, Dave was invited to share.

Dave and his wife Megan had spent many an hour in fellowship with my dad over the years and these were always very precious encounters with the Holy Spirit. It was no more than a few days before my dad was taken home to glory that he and Dave had apparently shared a most beautiful time of fellowship over the phone.

Dave recalls:-

"He was so excited and just couldn't wait to share two verses of scripture with me – Revelation 13:8 "...the Lamb (Jesus) slain from the foundation of the world." and Ephesians 1:4 "...He (God) hath chosen us in Him (Christ) before the foundation of the world.

Of course, these are very familiar verses and, over the years, we had been blessed many times as we shared our hearts together concerning them. But this was different. David was absolutely overwhelmed with joy at the miracle of God's love and grace towards the likes of us. It seemed that the Lord had taken him deeper than ever before into the fullness of His loving heart - it was a revelation! Words couldn't describe it, but David was bursting to overflowing with Life in the Spirit. And oh how we rejoiced in praise and worship as we joined together with all the company of heaven - hallelujah!"

What a thanksgiving service this was turning out to be with Pastor Dennis then preaching the Word.

My dad had surrendered his life to the Lord back in September 1967 and all of my life time he was up every morning at 5am, praying and seeking the Lord for the salvation of his family and others. He was a man who knew how to fight and often engaged in spiritual warfare.

Since I left London I had not seen my mum and dad that often, but my dad would write us a weekly letter, later to be addressed to Beth and Anna too. These were written every Sunday, arriving with us on a Tuesday, and were full of talk about the Lord. He would always close with a small paragraph for Beth and Anna.

Following my dad's death, my mum gave Steven and me a letter he had written to us both dated 16th January 2013, nine months before he left. The letter was a few pages long and was all about prayer. What a legacy to leave.

(This is the only chapter of this book, I have written with tears flowing.)

Believe the Words of the Prophets

Saturday 28th September 2013 was the last time I saw my dad – eighteen days before the Lord called him home.

He and my mum had travelled down to celebrate Anna's eighth birthday with us. Before heading back to London, he prophesied a scripture over my life:-

> *But on Mount Zion there shall be deliverance and there shall be holiness; the House of Jacob shall possess their possessions.*
> *(Obadiah 17)*

We did not go on to discuss this, as after all, this visit was to celebrate Anna's birthday. However, this word stuck with me and I have often meditated on it.

What a thought! Possess *my* possessions! To claim *my* inheritance, to at last hold what rightfully belongs to *me* in Christ for in Him dwells the fullness of the Godhead bodily, meaning I am complete in Him and have in Him all things that pertain to life and godliness. Why would I settle with a little deliverance, a little holiness and possessing just a little of *my* possessions?

In this context, Mount Zion is the place where God dwells among His people and His Name is known and the House of Jacob is the company of the redeemed of the Lord. The Lord offers and promises *total* deliverance, for it is His nature. He is a deliverer! This is something that we have to walk progressively into – just as the children of Israel took over the

Promised Land piece by piece and no single battle conquered the whole land. Too many of the redeemed are satisfied with deliverance from satan only and do not walk into newness of life, daily reckoning themselves dead indeed unto sin but alive unto God. They do not *possess their possessions*. If other children of God choose to live outside of their inheritance with no desire to *possess their possessions*, this was not going to stop me from pressing in and taking full possession of what was mine. This was my birthright and inheritance and I was coming hard after it. This would involve a dispossession; a forcing of someone to give something up.

The enemy of our souls hates the thought of even just one of God's children realising who they are in Christ.

In autumn 2019 I had been reading around Joshua and the spies going in and taking possession of the land. Ten out of the twelve spies showed little faith and gave a bad report about the land. They did not believe that God could help them, and the people as a whole were persuaded that it was not possible to take the land. Joshua and Caleb were the two spies who brought back a good report and believed that God would help them succeed. They were the only men from their generation permitted to go into the Promised Land after the time of wandering. Only two men from that generation fully entered the land.

The following scripture talks about being upheld by faith in the Lord but also about being established by faith in his prophets:-

> *Early in the morning they left for the Desert of Tekoa. As they set out, Jehoshaphat stood and said, "Listen to me, Judah and people of Jerusalem! Have faith in the Lord your God and you will be upheld; have faith in his prophets and you will be established."*
> *(2 Chronicles 20 v 20)*

For a season, my brother and his wife lived next door to neighbours who were a nuisance, and this started to affect their wellbeing. They both recall my dad telling them on 6th July 2013 that the Holy Spirit had told him that they would be moved into their new property twelve weeks to the day. He closed by saying to them that the test of this word would be whether it came to pass. 6th September 2013, they moved into their new home; twelve weeks exactly to the day. My dad got to see the fulfilment of the prophetic word he had brought before his home call and what a joy this must have been.

Now, six years on, the prophetic word he spoke over my life started to come to fruition, despite my dad not being here to see it.

Contend For Your Call

Now faith is confidence in what we hope for
and assurance about what we do not see.
(Hebrews 11 v 1)

When there is a call of God on your life, you can be confident that this *will* be contested. The enemy knows his time is short and will make every attempt to prevent you from fulfilling the mandate over your life. It is not your responsibility to convince others of the call on your life and your calling is validated by the results produced. When you have heard from God yourself, do not let people talk you down from your call.

Friday 29th August 2014, the end of the summer holidays spent in London with my mum, Beth and Anna, the first August without my dad. Knowing I was in London, Pastor Dennis came to visit and he prophesied over me:-

The Spirit of the Sovereign LORD is on me,
because the LORD has anointed me to
proclaim good news to the poor. He has sent
me to bind up the broken hearted, to proclaim
freedom for the captives and release from
darkness for the prisoners.
(Isaiah 61 v 1)

I also looked into the following verses:-

Is not this the kind of fasting I have chosen:
to loose the chains of injustice
and untie the cords of the yoke,

*to set the oppressed free
and break every yoke?
Is it not to share your food with the hungry
and to provide the poor
wanderer with shelter—
when you see the naked, to clothe them,
and not to turn away from your
own flesh and blood?
Then your light will break
forth like the dawn,
and your healing will quickly appear;
then your righteousness will go before you,
and the glory of the Lord
will be your rear guard.
Then you will call, and the Lord will answer;
you will cry for help, and he
will say: Here am I.
"If you do away with the yoke of oppression,
with the pointing finger and malicious talk,
and if you spend yourselves in
behalf of the hungry
and satisfy the needs of the oppressed,
then your light will rise in the darkness,
and your night will become like the noonday.
The Lord will guide you always;
he will satisfy your needs in a
sun-scorched land
and will strengthen your frame.
You will be like a well-watered garden,
like a spring whose waters never fail.
Your people will rebuild the ancient ruins
and will raise up the age-old foundations;*

you will be called Repairer of Broken Walls,
Restorer of Streets with Dwellings.
(Isaiah 58 v 6-12)

After prayer and seeking God with regard to this word spoken over me, I received another clear word from the Lord shortly after:-

"Lead my boys home"

When you know God has placed a specific call on your life, seek the Lord as to the fulfilment of the Word; there are people waiting for you to realise and fulfil your mandate.

When my dad was called home the previous year, I was never angry at God and there was always a peace over the family, even though we did not understand why he had to leave us so early, not even having met his fourth and youngest grandchild, 'little' David. I remember saying to God that I desired to have fruit for this loss.

Within the Walls

On a Wednesday in November 2015, I first stepped behind the walls of HMP Winchester, a Cat B men's prison, also accommodating young offenders over the age of 18. (This prison later appeared in the 2019 Channel 4 documentary '*Crime and Punishment*'.)

I had started volunteering with the Christian organisation, '*Prison Fellowship*' and was receiving training to become a facilitator on the '*Sycamore Tree*' course. The course is faith-based but *not* faith-promoting and is open to inmates of any or no faith and we as a team are not permitted to share our personal stories of faith with the inmates. Being part of this team requires regular commitment and attendance at a local prayer group. We also pray before and at the end of each session as a team, prior to the inmates arriving and after they have left.

Unless the LORD builds the house, the builders labour in vain.
(Psalm 127 v 1)

The Sycamore Tree programme is proven to change attitudes that contribute towards reoffending. The content of the programme is consistent with the pathways determined by the Her Majesty's Prison and Probation Service (HMPPS) to reduce reoffending. It is led by volunteers and is based on the principles of Restorative Justice and focuses on victim awareness. Participants are given the opportunity to explore the effects of their crimes on victims, offenders, and the community. We also discuss what it would mean for the offenders to take responsibility for their personal actions.

For the majority of learners on this six week course the most powerful session is week three, when a victim of crime comes in to talk about how crime has impacted their lives. Learners have an opportunity in the graduation ceremony on week six to express their remorse. HMP Winchester is one of the prisons that allow course participants to invite up to four family members or friends to attend the prison to witness their graduation. Our team of facilitators are also able to invite members of the community into the prison and everyone that comes in is extremely grateful for the experience. We all share lunch together and this involves any prison staff attending, including the Governor and probation officers. This is always a very significant day and it is wonderful to witness most of the participants, some with support, stand at the front and present their symbolic acts of restitution.

Having started to facilitate in HMP Winchester, it was not too long before I was approached to assist with a pilot programme in HMP Ford, a Cat D open prison. I soon started travelling to West Sussex to facilitate this, whilst still serving in Winchester.

Sadly there are *far* too many victims of crime that we could call upon to share their experiences first hand within the prison as part of our course. I have had the privilege of meeting just a few of these very special people who, despite their personal devastation and tragedy, somehow find it within themselves to want to share with offenders to help stop the creation of any new victims.

My family and I are personal friends of Ray and Vi Donovan who selflessly attend the prison and share about the tragic events surrounding the murder of their eighteen year old son and about how they met and forgave the boys who killed their precious Christopher.

On 24th February 2016, before heading into the prison I had lunch with Ray and Vi.

Vi writes:-

"I remember the day my husband and I met Fi for a pub lunch before going into Winchester prison.

We were talking about how she felt led by God to work with prisoners as she was a facilitator on the Sycamore Tree course at the time. Fi was not sure how that was going to happen, so there in the pub, we prayed into this, seeking God's guidance. During the prayer I remember telling Fi that I could actually see her holding the prisoners' hands.

While we were in the prison that afternoon I felt Fi had an overwhelming compassion for the men; this was very evident. We found out later that God opened a big door in her life and she was now helping to lead the Sycamore Tree course in the prison.

We have had the pleasure of not only taking part on the course as victims of crime, but watching Fi in some cases figuratively speaking 'holding the men's hands' as I had seen in the vision all those months ago! Fi was like a mother to the men; she helps and reassures them.

I feel blessed to have witnessed God fulfilling His word and the vision I had seen! What a privilege."

After a while, I trained to become a tutor in HMP Winchester and have not looked back since.

Throughout tutoring the course across the six weeks, I always ensure participants are told that what they have done does not define who they are. By the end of the course, everyone has been told and some now have a basic understanding that each one of them is of infinite worth and value and that they all have a destiny. Without a doubt, eyes start welling up and some heads become bowed, after all this news is very hard to swallow for many. I recall on one occasion, one inmate coming up to me at the end of a session and thanking me for telling him he had a worth, since he had never realised. We all have a life to live and all have issues of some description. Every family has been touched with some sort of struggle or difficulty. We have all made mistakes.

As someone once said, if you want to feel satan's wrath, just spend some time on his turf, talking to the people he keeps in bondage. Nothing makes satan angrier or more nervous than having one of God's people carry the flashlight of grace into the damp darkness of his dungeon. That is when he will fight the hardest and when we see the Holy Spirit shine most mightily. So many people have commented that my face literally *'lights up'* when I talk about my love for the prisoners and the work I do within the walls.

Shane Taylor, once known as *'one of the most dangerous prisoners in the UK'* is now also a family friend. He had been put away for attempted murder but then had his sentence extended as a result of attacking a prison officer. This dear brother has spent time in some of the most secure Cat A prisons and often in solitary confinement. Whilst in prison, he was radically transformed after an encounter with Jesus. Shane has been to our home a couple of times. I remember being sat chatting in the garden and he commented that from an ex-prisoner's perspective, it was blatant to him, that I had what it took to relate well to these boys. He said a prisoner will very quickly suss you out as to whether you are someone they can relate to. He said I definitely fell well within this *'category'*, so once again confirmation of the call on my life.

Sycamore Tree was the start, but I was shortly to have opportunities to serve "within the walls" that had nothing to do with Prison Fellowship.

Chapel Services – HMP Ford

During 2016/2017, I had the opportunity to visit HMP Ford with others from my church. We were invited here monthly to lead the Sunday evening service – a very different context to the work I had been doing with Prison Fellowship. Due to this being a cat D open prison it is also a very different experience to being within HMP Winchester.

As part of the service, our team would take turns to lead prayer, preach or share a testimony, as well as spending time praising and worshipping together with the inmates.

On occasions when I have prayed for inmates during these times I was told they could feel the power of the Holy Spirit on them. I also had the joy and honour of leading one young man to the Lord.

You Did it For Me

Bethan writes:-

"You really have touched so many people's lives! I think if all the prisoners and young people you have helped knew where you lived, you would have a queue of people waiting to see you!"

It would not be right for me to write this book without acknowledging that seeking to love and help broken people sometimes comes at a *significant* cost. These costs may be measured in time, money and emotions. A lot has happened over the last few years, way too much to go into, but this has involved me being called upon to provide support through mental breakdowns, huge grief and trauma as well as shopping, cooking and delivering meals daily to a young couple in need over a sustained period. I have counted this an honour and privilege.

From early 2019, things were emotionally very tough as we as a family were providing high levels of support for that young couple; myself in particular. During this season, I had to work through the realisation that something very weighty I had been told a few years previously was now exposed as a lie.

Over the next few months, in order to protect my own sanity and mental wellbeing, I acquired some large sheets of paper and wrote things down. This went some way in helping me process things but I knew deep down that I needed someone to pray with me and this needed to be soon.

I made contact with Pastor Andrew who kindly arranged for me to see him that next day. Upon arrival, I poured out my heart to him and, many tissues later, we got to prayer and broke off the lies that had been told both to me and about me and any trauma or curse that the enemy had sought to introduce through this channel. By the time I left, I knew that business had been done and the Holy Spirit had worked in deep places that only He could reach. I forgave this person and as a result, freedom followed. The love and compassion I have always had for this individual far outweighed any hurt or damage that had been caused to me and my family. I remained fully committed to doing all I could to be there and continue to support.

The families of some of the young people we have supported *could not* and *will never* understand and realise the depths of what we as a family have gone through in trying to help care and provide for their own flesh and blood. Thank God for His amazing grace which once again, goes further still, resulting in forgiveness. There is no waste in God.

> *Then the King will say to those on his right,*
> *'Come, you who are blessed by my Father;*
> *take your inheritance, the kingdom prepared*
> *for you since the creation of the world. For I*
> *was hungry and you gave me something to*
> *eat, I was thirsty and you gave me something*
> *to drink, I was a stranger and you invited me*
> *in, I needed clothes and you clothed me, I was*
> *sick and you looked after me, I was in prison*
> *and you came to visit me.'*

"Then the righteous will answer him, 'Lord, when did we see you hungry and feed you, or thirsty and give you something to drink? When did we see you a stranger and invite you in, or needing clothes and clothe you? When did we see you sick or in prison and go to visit you?'

"The King will reply, 'Truly I tell you, whatever you did for one of the least of these brothers and sisters of mine, you did for me.'

(Matthew 25 v 34-40)

Josh writes:-

"During the summer of 2016 I was living in a homeless shelter in the worse state ever as a result of my spice addiction. I was coming to the point of life and death with my emotional wellbeing leading me towards suicide. I met Fi during this period and she showed me hope and introduced me to her family. Subsequently I moved in with them not long after. Whilst living with them, I got the best job I had ever had, successfully ran two half marathons, one of which was for charity and most importantly I got my body into the fittest state it had ever been in. Unfortunately shortly later, I suffered a severe motorbike accident in which Fi and Pete looked after me and through God's guidance and blessings, I had a rapid recovery.

A lot happened during my stay with Fi and her family and they have all showed me what unconditional love and true forgiveness is and for this I am very grateful.

It is now years later and because of the impact Fi had had on my life, myself and my previous partner decided to make her godmother to my son, who is now with the angels. Nonetheless, I felt the role of godmother was suited to no one other than Fi as there is not one person I would have trusted more to look after my little man (Fi was honoured). Her impact on my life has been huge and I have experienced her non judgmental love and care which comes from her passionate walk of faith with Jesus, a true inspiration to all."

As will be apparent from what Josh has written above, he and our family have been through a lot together, good and bad. We have shared many a laugh, in particular, one time when Josh locked me in the garden with the hosepipe fully loaded with no way of me re-entering the house without being soaked. Then there was the time we all went to the local pantomime. I needed the toilet prior to the interval and politely asked Josh to please move so I could get across without causing unnecessary disruption. He refused to move, pretending to have not heard, leaving me with no option but to literally climb over him – much to his amusement.

On a significantly more serious note and, as Josh has mentioned, we have cared for him following a serious accident, starting with me meeting him in resus. I have also walked with him through further extremely traumatic life events.

Rebekah writes:-

"I have known Fi for about sixteen years as a close friend and over the last four years have been blown away by how God has used her and her family and put on her heart a real compassion and empathy for offenders and the homeless.

Fi and I have had many discussions over the years and I have been really struck by how God has used the most unlikely person to do His most remarkable work through her.

I am often reminded of the unlikelihood of David and Goliath and how God used David in that situation and of an image of a kitten looking back at his reflection and seeing a lion. My lovely friend may be petite in stature, but what a giant she is in her service for God. The fact that God has chosen her to work and speak into the lives and hearts of these quite often large and on occasion, historically violent young men is quite remarkable.

I have also witnessed firsthand the personal cost at which this service has come to her and her family. I have seen it affect her emotionally, spiritually and financially as she has not only opened up her heart but she and her family have also opened up their home.

I have also seen how God has worked through all that with Fi and has brought her comfort, wisdom, forgiveness and reassurance that she is doing exactly the work that God has called her too and how pleased God is with her for her obedience to Him."

Going to the Other Side

On Sunday 24th November, we had a visiting preacher, Bishop Don Carpenter. He delivered what would turn out to be *another* prophetic word. The portion of scripture Don was speaking from was:-

> *That day when evening came, he said to his disciples, "Let us go over to the other side."*
> *Leaving the crowd behind, they took him along, just as he was, in the boat. There were also other boats with him. A furious squall came up, and the waves broke over the boat, so that it was nearly swamped. Jesus was in the stern, sleeping on a cushion. The disciples woke him and said to him, "Teacher, don't you care if we drown?"*
>
> *He got up, rebuked the wind and said to the waves, "Quiet! Be still!" Then the wind died down and it was completely calm.*
>
> *He said to his disciples, "Why are you so afraid? Do you still have no faith?"*
>
> *They were terrified and asked each other, "Who is this? Even the wind and the waves obey him!"*
>
> *(Mark 4 v 35-41)*

Bishop Don went on to talk about the other side *being* the destination and going to the other side *not* being up for debate. After inviting Jesus into your heart, you give up the right to navigate your own course through life and instead submit to your Heavenly Father, saying, *"Not my will, but yours be done."* Because I followed Jesus and obeyed Him, many lives have been touched.

I remember Don giving a beautiful example of how an earthly father steps out onto thick hazardous ice. The father walks a little further onto the ice, showing it to be safe and then reaches out his hand to his child to take hold. The father has gone ahead of the child and the child can confidently follow without fear holding tightly onto the hand of his father.

An old song comes to mind as I am sat writing. This song was playing when Anna came into the world back in 2005:-

Tis so sweet to trust in Jesus,
Just to take Him at His Word
Just to rest upon His promise,
Just to know, "Thus saith the Lord!"

Jesus, Jesus, how I trust Him!
How I've proved Him o'er and o'er
Jesus, Jesus, precious Jesus!
Oh, for grace to trust Him more!

I'm so glad I learned to trust Him,
Precious Jesus, Saviour, Friend
And I know that He is with me,
Will be with me to the end.

Oh, how sweet to trust in Jesus,
Just to trust His cleansing blood
And in simple faith to plunge me
'Neath the healing, cleansing flood!

Yes, 'tis sweet to trust in Jesus,
Just from sin and self to cease
Just from Jesus simply taking
Life and rest, and joy and peace...

Anointed and Appointed

***The thief comes only to steal and kill and
destroy; I have come that they may have life,
and have it to the full.
(John 10 v 10)***

Wednesday 27th November 2019, I attended the
prison to conduct peer mentor training. Once we had
completed all the necessary paperwork, my new
recruit and I had some spare time before he was due
to be collected and returned to his cell. So over tea
and biscuits, (*always a popular luxury*), we spent
some time chatting about his past and the struggles
that he felt he would potentially face upon his
eventual release from HMPS. With no prompting
from me, he opened his heart up and started speaking
from a deep place. As long as I have worked in
prisons I still find even if I can harden myself to the
tragic back stories while I am there, I often break once
I am off site.

Before leaving, one of the chaplains said one of my
more experienced peer mentors had heard I was on
site and wondered whether it would be okay for him
to come and sit with us for a while. Of course I said
yes, always being pleased to see previous recruits; it
is so nice to catch up and see how they are doing post
Sycamore Tree. Through my association with HMP
Winchester and through attending chapel services
from time to time, I know and recognise many faces
across the establishment, both in terms of inmates and
staff.

When I returned home that evening, something very significant happened. I started weeping over the man I had trained that afternoon and knew deep within, that something else lay ahead for me with respect to these boys; *His boys*. I explained how I was feeling to Pete and he witnessed what I was expressing. I do not know *fully* what this "something else" involves, only that it involves continuing to work alongside prisoners and ex-offenders. I will continue to yield to the Holy Spirit and allow this to be revealed in His perfect timing. The events of this day and the sense I had that there was so much more to come were to take on even greater significance the following day, as I was lifted out of my car, and laid in the road, before being blue-lighted to Southampton General.

The Confrontation

A&E was an all-too-familiar environment since, over the last few years, I had been here once with Pete and once with one of the young men who lived with us, after he was attacked. I also had the privilege of spending many hours supporting and caring for Josh following his accident.

I don't remember much about the journey apart from the speed of travel and the siren – not a pleasant experience while drifting in and out of consciousness. I have a vague recollection of being shifted from the ambulance and then lying on a bed somewhere in a corridor.

The cords of death entangled me;
the torrents of destruction overwhelmed me.
The cords of the grave coiled around me;
the snares of death confronted me.
They confronted me in the day of my disaster
(and came upon me),
but the Lord was my support.
(Psalm 18 v 4 – 5, 18)

Whilst sat alone in the corridor on *'just another Thursday'*, I knew deep in my spirit that God was going to have me walk *through* a valley. It was like He had scooped me up and cocooned me safely with Him and this was to become my daily experience. This *plot 'to take me out'* would not succeed but would be used for the glory of God and for the extension of His Kingdom. This was not about me. We often sing *'Jesus at the Centre of it all'* and this

47

was definitely going to be the case. I had heard and listened to the voice of my Saviour and refused to be distracted or diverted by giving any attention to any other voice.

Before Pete arrived, I was moved to a bay but due to an ongoing norovirus outbreak, he had difficulty getting past the external waiting area. I remember just wanting him to be there and eventually, recognising the severity of the situation, a nurse graciously allowed him through.

My recollection of what happened next is limited but Pete tells me various professionals visited to test my abilities. This involved me holding their hands as tightly as I could and pushing my legs against them to gauge my strength. At this stage, it was evident to them that my left side was substantially weaker than my right.

In this period of waiting, and even *before* any test results, I received a message from Pastor Andrew shortly after 17:30pm in which he assured me that he had been praying for me since he had heard the news and his message went on to say:-

"This is the Word of the Lord Unto You:-"

"You shall make a full and complete recovery. It shall be as if it never happened. You are every part completely whole."

The Holy Spirit had assured me directly earlier whilst sat alone and now this had been backed up. Victory was assured on day one of this adventure of faith through the valley; my Father had gone ahead.

A couple of hours later I made the first of many trips to the scanner. A CT scan quickly revealed a growth sent from the pit of hell, behind by right eye. The nurse who informed us of the medics' findings, was a Christian who we knew. I remember her pulling the curtain around the area we were sat and praying. Pete then sorted us both some food as I had not eaten or drank all day and, by this point, we were both starting to feel it.

The medics informed me that I would be unable to drive for a year as a result of having had a seizure (*driving being an essential part of my job*). They also said they thought the growth had metastasised from a tumour elsewhere – so a second trip to the scanner was booked for the next day, this time for an MRI. In any case, they told me they wanted me to stay in overnight for close monitoring.

Pastor Andrew had sent me a message confirming he would come and pray with us on the Friday morning and also encouraged me to listen to the doctors and cooperate with them BUT to reject every diagnosis that did not pertain unto LIFE.

He reminded me to be strong and *very* courageous and then sent me through a video filled with verses of scripture relating to healing and suggested I *'take three times a day like medicine'*. This was wonderful and reminded me of my dad. When I had struggled in my health all those years ago, my dad had typed up a list of scriptures and told me to take *'three a day'* like medicine. He had also added the comment, *'if little improvement, double the dose'*.

Pastor Andrew told me to arrest fear, pull down doubt, and stand in my authority as a daughter of God. He reminded me that this *'thing'* had no right to be in my body and it *would* be expelled in Jesus Name.

The next stop was a bed in the acute medical unit (AMU) on the right hand side near to a window as I required constant monitoring. I had been in various departments through the night when supporting Josh but this time *I* would be the one wearing pyjamas and being completely dependent.

It was always me running around chasing doctors up for news and making sure there were sufficient drinks and snacks and home comforts; I was the one who was supposed to make sure all was well and provide a hand to hold and a shoulder to cry on; I was the one who sought to bring calm when panic had set in... after all, this was what normally happened all the previous times I had been here...

Pete and I chatted and made a list of all the things I would need from home. Shortly after he had left, I remember feeling another seizure coming on; this time very much stronger; very dark and definitely *'not'* my portion. This was very frightening with my whole body almost preparing for what it knew was on the way. I just managed to cry out for help before losing consciousness for the second time in my lifetime. I recall at least three professionals running across to assist me and gather they acted very quickly to provide the necessary anti-seizure medication intravenously.

Once I regained consciousness, I found myself in bed six in the high observation area of the AMU. Because episode two was much more intense, I was now drugged up to the eyeballs to reduce swelling and to calm my brain down. I had lost movement on my left side and had become completely paranoid due to my brain being in a state of shock. This experience gave me *just* a glimpse of what living with paranoia must be like: deeply unpleasant. Many of the people I support, in and out of the prison environment, suffer with this day in, day out; it is one of the many chains the enemy uses to keep people locked and bound.

At approximately 10:30pm, Pete arrived back at the hospital to find me in a much worse state; my ability to move having significantly deteriorated. After settling me for the night, Pete returned home. I am so grateful to God that he spared my husband from witnessing me suffering both seizures as I expect they would have been very traumatic to witness, not easy to get out of your head.

As a result of a faulty call button, I had to shout every time I needed assistance, which was at least every half an hour. In the normal run of things, one would feel bad about shouting through the night but it was almost a case of '*if you can't beat them, join them.*' I expect most, if not all other buzzers were working as the '*beeps*' became another all-too-familiar noise. This was alongside lights being on all night long and background music on loop.

The paralysis of my left side and the broken buzzer added to the frustration and upset. I would lay on my right hand side and try resting my left arm on the side of my body but this would simply just drop off again. The nurses were called across on a regular basis to cover me up, pass my lip balm and sort me with drinks; most likely, taking a deep breath and bracing themselves to remain polite on each fresh call.

The nurses' station was in sight and I was aware that my temperature, blood pressure, pulse and breathing rate were all being monitored *very* closely. I recall the machine I was linked up to causing alarm at one point but having been examined, things were clearly being managed their end.

Due to the temporary paranoia, I remember taking a dislike to one of the nurses. When it came to having to deal with the number of cannulas and needles I had already experienced in such a short duration, I was starting to get upset and the lack of sleep was not helping. God knew what was required for the next cannula change and in came a new young nurse who stepped in and made all the difference after a first '*very dark*' night. Compassion and gentleness flowed from this man and he was '*just what the doctor ordered'*. As unpleasant as these necessary procedures are, this nurse sorted the cannula and everything else in a tender way, causing as little discomfort as he could.

On Friday morning Pete arrived back at 9am. After him showering me, we awaited the arrival of Pastor Andrew due at 11am. I remember being laid out in the bed, most likely looking terrible but not caring – after all, it comes with a Pastor's territory and he would be used to seeing people in worse states. I recall him sitting to my left and Pete on my right. We prayed and had communion together. I remember nothing else about this visit.

The devil had not liked this time of fellowship and intimacy with Christ with us sharing communion, the three of us having come into agreement for complete healing. Unsurprisingly, the enemy attempted to bid for attention as soon as Pastor Andrew had left. I recall almost immediately a very dark voice speaking and it said: *"I can tell you something about that priest...!"* I had never heard a voice like that before; it was unwelcome and stank of hell itself; a voice to silence and take authority over.

My sheep listen to my voice; I know them, and they follow me. I give them eternal life, and they shall never perish; no one will snatch them out of my hand. My Father, who has given them to me, is greater than all; no one can snatch them out of my Father's hand. I and the Father are one.
(John 10:27-30)

Earlier that day, I had heard the voice of my Shepherd and Father, a gentle yet authoritative voice. Due to the shocked state of my brain, I was hallucinating. Another unknown voice then attempted to speak, this time trying to mock *me* and said something like... *"Isn't that the woman who drives a big bus around; always trying to help people...?"* I thought these were the voices of people in the ward sitting chatting with their relatives, or even staff. It was only after the effects of the meds had lessened that I realised these voices had been demonic.

As the day progressed, I moved to a chair and Pete and I mostly sat around waiting for professionals to visit and provide updates.

Pete and I have a friend of the family, Sean, another Christian who works within the Neurological department. Sean had heard about the situation and made contact with Pete. He called in briefly whilst on shift to assure us he was there if we needed anything; another gift of grace.

It was shortly time to enter the MRI scanner for a thorough search.

For you created my inmost being;
you knit me together in my mother's womb.
I praise you because I am fearfully and
wonderfully made;
your works are wonderful,
I know that full well.
My frame was not hidden from you
when I was made in the secret place,
when I was woven together in the depths of
the earth.
Your eyes saw my unformed body;
all the days ordained for me were written in
your book
before one of them came to be.
(Psalm 139 v 13-16)

According to the infallible Word of God, my brain had been formed perfectly and any *'intruder'* seeking to defy this Truth was due for immediate eviction. I had the mind of Christ!

I have never known anybody to live up to their name as much as my very precious sister, *Faith*. I do believe that I would not be the woman of faith *I* am today, if it had not been partly due to this woman's influence in my life. Pete informs me that Faith came to visit me the next day and we spent most of the time in prayer. I remember requesting she visit and also recall constantly asking Pete about her imminent arrival but do not recall anything more.

Pete once again stayed and got me ready for what would be another sleepless night in an unpleasant and oppressive environment.

But I Have Lunch @ 1pm...

We take so much for granted when life is just ticking on. The previous Saturday, Pete had spent the day with Beth and Anna and some work colleagues, walking and enjoying lunch in the New Forest. Meanwhile, I had started Christmas *'browsing'* with my mum for anything that caught my eye for Pete or other family members. One thing I *had* to sort that day was the obligatory secret Santa gift for my allocated work colleague. The team had been invited to take on the challenge of purchasing a gift beginning with the letter of the individual's first name. What do you buy for a young man whose name begins with *'M'*? Determined to avoid the obvious chocolate items, I was delighted to stumble across a *'Mr Manly Hair and Body Wash'*. I was also pleased to find some suitable gifts for both the young men who had lived with us and for their partners.

Within a week, I had gone from driving around town at my leisure, to now being completely dependent on people to help me. However, I had complete assurance of certain imminent and complete victory *through* my God; my Alpha and Omega was in full control.

This Saturday lunchtime, Pete and I had been due at a Sycamore Tree team meal which I had organised a couple of months earlier as a pre-Christmas celebration. This was also the first meal I had invited the chaplaincy team to attend and Reverend Cliff McClelland had joined the party, Senior Chaplain David Hinks being unable but grateful to have been asked. The fact I had invited the chaplaincy team to join us highlights the strength of relationship between us.

Anna had made name settings for everyone at my request and I had printed off a reminder of the pre-ordered meals for people which were carefully stuck inside. The week running up to the meal, people had dropped out for various reasons but we were definitely going to be there… after all I had organised it.

Pete had contacted the team to explain we could unfortunately not be present and was respectfully asked whether the meal should be cancelled, given the circumstances. Pete knew my response would be for them to press ahead without me and so they did and apparently had a great time, although clearly missed us.

Pete was due back in to see me as early as permitted but reminds me that I called him very early that morning in floods of tears, very distraught after a second night of no sleep. Exhaustion had started to take a toll. Pete arrived a while later, accompanied by an egg and cheese muffin, hash brown and regular tea – the familiar comforting aroma of McDonalds being a *'go to'* in times of high stress.

Breakfast was followed by another accompanied trip to the shower with the added complication of having my hair washed. This was followed by the nurse I liked doing the rounds and asking me to attempt to move my left hand and arm. I recall becoming really upset as I realised that I simply could not get it to do anything. Tears flowed and Pete assured me I was doing really well and that he was proud of me. Whilst this nurse was off doing his rounds, Pete talked me through some gentle attempts at getting the left hand working again. I would sit in the armchair resting my hand on a pillow and Pete would ask me to wiggle my fingers. This was such hard work. Then to lift my hand slightly off the pillow – next to impossible. The hardest challenge of all was getting my hand to turn over. These *simple* movements were now taking all the strength I had and this was very distressing for us both. One day enjoying life to the max and now in almost a blink of an eye, caught in a place of severe disability.

I remember there being approximately a ten second delay between me telling my hand to move and seeing it respond. I knew *what* to do and *how* to do it but could not do it and I remember getting stressed and worn out. Eventually, I managed to muster up enough strength to '*perform*' and we called the nurse back over to show him how things had improved. He was clearly pleased to see that *I* was encouraged. I had also regained some movement in my left leg which was an encouraging sign and Pete said in true *'Fi style'*, I had started marching around the ward...

A ward assistant sat with us for close to an hour, tensions were high and both Pete and I were physically, mentally and emotionally exhausted. They always say hospital environments are the worst place to recover as sleep deprivation hits hard. This lady too was a grace gift. She could see we were struggling and sensitively shielded us by pulling the curtains. She was encouraging and provided a listening ear as well as talking me through an increasingly complex set of exercises to retrain my fragile brain and recover the strength in my arm. By the time she left, I had started to regain motion.

Eventually two occupational therapists visited to see whether heading home was an option. After managing some stairs, I was given the green light by the consultant who discharged me to return as an outpatient for what was to follow.

Excited about heading home and being reunited with my family, (having last seen Beth and Anna briefly two mornings ago), we then faced a delay whilst waiting for the necessary meds to be dispensed. Finally, it was time for Pete to locate a wheelchair as this was the *only* way I was getting to the car.

The days following this were spent re-adjusting at home, regaining my movement and rebuilding my confidence. I remember playing catch with a small ball with my mum using my left hand and being so pleased (especially with being a right hander). The stairs were a breeze from early on although spatial awareness was somewhat of an issue initially – forcing me to be even more determined. I would turn on the tap with my right hand but fail to bring my left hand anywhere near the tap. I also knocked into a wall or two along the way but this soon passed. Pete ran things for the month of December and for this I remain truly grateful. God knew what He was doing when He put us together.

It May Look Like I'm Surrounded

On 3rd December, I sent this message to Steven:-

"I have been dancing on the devil's head!"

The following day we started planning a prayer meeting at our home, Steven's summary of the plan was:-

"We do not gather as thermometers to measure the temperature and mull over detail; we gather as thermostats to change the temperature and fix the climate."

The following portion of scripture has always been a favourite of mine:-

After this, the Moabites and Ammonites with some of the Meunites came to wage war against Jehoshaphat.

Some people came and told Jehoshaphat, "A vast army is coming against you from Edom, from the other side of the Dead Sea. It is already in Hazezon Tamar" (that is, En Gedi). Alarmed, Jehoshaphat resolved to inquire of the Lord, and he proclaimed a fast for all Judah. The people of Judah came together to seek help from the Lord; indeed, they came from every town in Judah to seek him.

Then Jehoshaphat stood up in the assembly of Judah and Jerusalem at the temple of the

*Lord in the front of the new courtyard
and said:*

*"Lord, the God of our ancestors, are you not
the God who is in heaven? You rule over all
the kingdoms of the nations. Power and might
are in your hand, and no one can withstand
you. Our God, did you not drive out the
inhabitants of this land before your people
Israel and give it forever to the descendants of
Abraham your friend? They have lived in it
and have built in it a sanctuary for your
Name, saying, 'If calamity comes upon us,
whether the sword of judgment, or plague or
famine, we will stand in your presence before
this temple that bears your Name and will cry
out to you in our distress, and you will hear
us and save us.'*

*"But now here are men from Ammon, Moab
and Mount Seir, whose territory you would
not allow Israel to invade when they came
from Egypt; so they turned away from them
and did not destroy them. See how they are
repaying us by coming to drive us out of the
possession you gave us as an inheritance. Our
God, will you not judge them? For we have
no power to face this vast army that is
attacking us. We do not know what to do, but
our eyes are on you."*

*All the men of Judah, with their wives and
children and little ones, stood there
before the Lord.*

61

Then the Spirit of the Lord came on Jahaziel son of Zechariah, the son of Benaiah, the son of Jeiel, the son of Mattaniah, a Levite and descendant of Asaph, as he stood in the assembly.

He said: "Listen, King Jehoshaphat and all who live in Judah and Jerusalem! This is what the Lord says to you: 'Do not be afraid or discouraged because of this vast army. For the battle is not yours, but God's. Tomorrow march down against them. They will be climbing up by the Pass of Ziz, and you will find them at the end of the gorge in the Desert of Jeruel. You will not have to fight this battle. Take up your positions; stand firm and see the deliverance the Lord will give you, Judah and Jerusalem. Do not be afraid; do not be discouraged. Go out to face them tomorrow, and the Lord will be with you.'"

Jehoshaphat bowed down with his face to the ground, and all the people of Judah and Jerusalem fell down in worship before the Lord. Then some Levites from the Kohathites and Korahites stood up and praised the Lord, the God of Israel, with a very loud voice.

Early in the morning they left for the Desert of Tekoa. As they set out, Jehoshaphat stood and said, "Listen to me, Judah and people of Jerusalem! Have faith in the Lord your God and you will be upheld; have faith in his prophets and you will be successful." After consulting the people, Jehoshaphat appointed men to sing to the Lord and to praise him for the splendour of his holiness as they went out at the head of the army, saying:

"Give thanks to the Lord, for his love endures forever."

As they began to sing and praise, the Lord set ambushes against the men of Ammon and Moab and Mount Seir who were invading Judah, and they were defeated. The Ammonites and Moabites rose up against the men from Mount Seir to destroy and annihilate them. After they finished slaughtering the men from Seir, they helped to destroy one another.

When the men of Judah came to the place that overlooks the desert and looked toward the vast army, they saw only dead bodies lying on the ground; no one had escaped. So Jehoshaphat and his men went to carry off their plunder, and they found among them a great amount of equipment and clothing and also articles of value—more than they could take away. There was so much plunder that it took three days to collect it. On the fourth day they assembled in the Valley of Berakah, where they praised the Lord. This is why it is called the Valley of Berakah to this day.

Then, led by Jehoshaphat, all the men of Judah and Jerusalem returned joyfully to Jerusalem, for the Lord had given them cause

*to rejoice over their enemies. They entered
Jerusalem and went to the temple of the Lord
with harps and lyres and trumpets.*

*The fear of God came on all the surrounding
kingdoms when they heard how the Lord had
fought against the enemies of Israel. And the
kingdom of Jehoshaphat was at peace, for his
God had given him rest on every side."*

(2 Chronicles 20)

It was time to go on the offensive. The enemy had launched an attack attempting to put an end to the call of God on my life, aware of the threat this posed to his kingdom. As children of the Most High God it was time to announce full scale war on the kingdom of darkness.

Pete knocked next door to let our neighbours know that we would be having a prayer meeting and that it would most likely be loud. The evening of Thursday 5th December was set aside for praise, communion and intercession in our home. Pete, myself, my mum, Steven, his wife Lottie and my dear sister Faith gathered together. I had also invited another fellow warrior, my sister Elaine, but she had car trouble so prayed alongside us at home. People from my brother's church in London had committed to pray along then too.

When Elaine and I had fellowshipped on the phone, she reminded me that my dad had been a mighty man of God and that together with my mum, they had raised myself and my brother to become *'mighty warriors, pace setters and territory takers'*.

Truly I tell you, whatever you bind on earth
will be bound in heaven, and whatever you
loose on earth will be loosed in heaven.
Again, truly I tell you that if two of you on
earth agree about anything they ask for, it
will be done for them by my Father in heaven.
For where two or three gather in my name,
there am I with them.
(Matthew 18 v 18-20)

When the praises started to go up, the glory starting to descend. Both Steven and Faith discerned a moment where something shifted in the spiritual realm. This was just the start. We had laid hold of God and He had responded. He had not been passive, He heard *and* He moved. Convinced of this, what attempted to present as a daunting line up of appointments, would now be approached from that platform; Heaven's song drowning out every other narrative. Hallelujah!

In my distress I called to the Lord;
I cried to my God for help.
From his temple he heard my voice;
my cry came before him, into his ears.
The earth trembled and quaked,
and the foundations of the mountains shook;
they trembled because he was angry.
Smoke rose from his nostrils;
consuming fire came from his mouth,
burning coals blazed out of it.

He parted the heavens and came down;
dark clouds were under his feet.
He mounted the cherubim and flew;
he soared on the wings of the wind.
He made darkness his covering, his
canopy around him—
the dark rain clouds of the sky.
Out of the brightness of his presence
clouds advanced,
with hailstones and bolts of lightning.
The Lord thundered from heaven;
the voice of the Most High resounded.
He shot his arrows and scattered the enemy,
with great bolts of lightning he routed them.
The valleys of the sea were exposed
and the foundations of the earth laid bare
at your rebuke, Lord,
at the blast of breath from your nostrils.
(Psalm 18 v 6-15)

Steven writes:-

"The soul that on Jesus doth lean for repose
He will not He will not desert to its foes
The soul that all hell should endeavour to shake
He'll never, no never, no never forsake"

"On Thursday 5th December 2019, my wife and I
left South East London around 4:30pm to drive to
my sister's house for a prayer meeting. A week ago
she had experienced a seizure while driving and
after being scanned the hospital had identified a
suspected brain tumour. We had been invited to

come down and agree with her in prayer for complete deliverance.

On arrival we found my sister lucid and alert and up on her feet excited and expectant to be gathering to pray. We spent time in worship together and called on the Name of the Lord. During this time the tangible presence of God came and beyond any shadow of a doubt, we called on His kingdom to come in its fullness and from this early stage business was transacted.

The tone had been set and the context had been fixed. This was not to be a journey of defeat and settling down into diagnosis, prognosis and resignation. The Name of The Lord is a strong tower. The righteous run into it and they are saved. There was an expectation that God was going to reveal His Mighty Hand and do that which only He could do. This was not a season in which to be coming under a settlement with circumstance but a time to be laying hold of God."

A day later I had regained all movement down my left hand side and was up, dancing and praising. I remember, even at this early stage, testifying to being at complete peace and filled with joy.

Steven confirmed there had been a shift in the spiritual realm and went on to say:-

"The goodness of God has been revealed, is being revealed and will be revealed."

The Tightrope and His Amazing Grace

This journey was not for the faint-hearted and was going to require a steely-eyed endurance.

Because the Sovereign Lord helps me,
I will not be disgraced.
Therefore have I set my face like flint,
and I know I will not be put to shame.
(Isaiah 50 v 7)

A sister had seen a vision on 7th December which happened to be the day Pete and I attended the hospital for a further CT scan. This sister wrote down what she had received from the Holy Spirit and then sent it to me. Whilst seeking the Lord and interceding for me, she had seen in the spirit, two mountains and an enormous chasm with a tightrope between the mountains. One mountain was big but the destination mountain was *enormous*.

When someone gives you a word, it is important to weigh it. This word summed up exactly how the Holy Spirit had positioned me and revealed to me the way I would need to walk this one through. In order to remain on the tightrope, focus was essential. Failure to look straight ahead at *all* times would result in my senses being overwhelmed.

You have given plenty of room for my steps
under me that my feet did not slip.
(Psalm 18 v 36)

This tightrope *could* be crossed but this was *only* possible in *His* power and by *His* Spirit.

'Not by might nor by power, but by my Spirit,'
says the Lord Almighty. "What are you,
mighty mountain? Before Zerubbabel you
will become level ground. Then he will bring
out the capstone to shouts of 'God bless it!
God bless it!'" Then the word of the Lord
came to me: "The hands of Zerubbabel have
laid the foundation of this temple; his hands
will also complete it. Then you will know that
the Lord Almighty has sent me to you."
(Zechariah 4 v 6-9)

Pete was unable to walk this *'tightrope adventure'* for me or even *with* me in fullness but as my spiritual covering, had to watch and pray.

The prayer of a righteous man is powerful
and effective.
(James 5 v 16)

I would not have chosen to travel this route or to have my family have to watch me walk the rope. However, I have said to Pete throughout this journey, that I would not exchange it. It was all for God's glory alone and for the extension of His Kingdom. The closeness I now have with the Holy Spirit is not something I would trade.

Taste and see that the Lord is good; blessed is
the one who takes refuge in Him.
(Psalm 34 v 8)

The fact that Pete has not been able to walk the rope with me has obviously brought with it some challenges, but there has been sufficient grace for each new day and on occasions this has been *felt* moment by moment.

Failed Enemy Assignment

On Saturday 7th December we had an early start to arrive at the hospital for a full body CT scan at 8:45am. I recognised the lady stood smiling at the side of the machine but could not place her until later. It turns out she was Verji, a sister from church and a specialist radiographer. Another blessing from God on a day when He knew I needed a little encouragement.

The nurse who had prepped me for the scan had unfortunately used so much tape on my hand that when she attempted to remove it, the skin was sore and I became upset; removing the tape was worse than the cannula insertion or removal. I guess it was just one of those days we all hit from time to time and cannot explain, when the little things push us close to our limits.

(The outcome of this full body scan highlighted a 'suspicious area' which needed further investigation resulting in me having to endure a gastroscopy and biopsy. Praise the Lord, it was concluded that this area, although not as it should be, could be left alone with no further action required).

On Sunday 8th December my mum drove me to church. The last time we had been there was two weeks earlier, when Bishop Don Carpenter had spoken powerfully about going to the other side. This week, Pastor Andrew had been speaking about not doing a deal with the devil and about not coming to terms with situations but, instead, overcoming them in Jesus' Name.

My mum and I were called forward at the end of the meeting for prayer, two chairs having been especially placed at the front. Pastor Andrew explained briefly to everyone, that ten days earlier, I had suffered a seizure while driving and the medics had pronounced a brain tumour over my life. He then went on to say:-

"BUT we are announcing life in the Name of Jesus!"

Before praying, the worship team led us all in the song *"Yes and Amen"*:-

> *Father of kindness*
> *You have poured out of grace*
> *You brought me out of darkness*
> *You have filled me with peace*
> *Giver of mercy*
> *You're my help in time of need*
> *Lord I can't help but sing*

By the time we had reached *this* point in the song, I had jumped up out of my seat and stood with my arms raised high, rejoicing. God had remembered His promise and divine health was my portion. We went on to sing...

> *Faithful You are*
> *Faithful forever You will be*
> *Faithful You are*
> *All Your promises are yes and Amen*
> *All Your promises are yes and Amen*

Beautiful Saviour
You have brought me near
You pulled me from the ashes
You have broken every curse
Blessed Redeemer
You have set this captive free
Lord I can't help but sing

Faithful You are
Faithful forever You will be
Faithful You are
All Your promises are yes and Amen

Everyone then joined hands *and* their faith and began to decree and declare the blessing and goodness of God over my life. Pastors Ron and Margaret were then called to anoint me with oil in accordance with the scripture:-

Is anyone among you in trouble? Let them pray. Is anyone happy? Let them sing songs of praise. Is anyone among you sick? Let them call the elders of the church to pray over them and anoint them with oil in the name of the Lord. And the prayer offered in faith will make the sick person well; the Lord will raise them up. If they have sinned, they will be forgiven. Therefore confess your sins to each other and pray for each other so that you may be healed. The prayer of a righteous person is powerful and effective.
(James 5 v 13-16)

Pastor Ron then gave me the following verses:-

> *Because of the Lord's great love we are not*
> *consumed, for His compassions never fail.*
> *They are new every morning; great is your*
> *faithfulness. I say to myself, the Lord is my*
> *portion; therefore I will wait for Him." The*
> *Lord is good to those whose hope is in Him, to*
> *the one who seeks Him; it is good to wait*
> *quietly for the salvation of the Lord.*
> *(Lamentations 3 v 22-26)*

Pastor Ron emphasised that because of the Lord's mercies, I would not be consumed and that this was the Word of the Lord to me.

Pastor Margaret then prayed thanking the Lord that He had my life held in the palm of His hand and she felt Him put a blanket of love around me. She thanked the Lord for giving me the assurance that all was *and* would remain well. The whole congregation came into agreement and the joy of the Lord filled the place.

Pastor Margaret later gave me the scripture:-

> *Before I formed you in the womb I knew you,*
> *before you were born I set you apart;*
> *I appointed you as a prophet to the nations.*
> *(Jeremiah 1 v 5)*

After prayer, we went on and sang the final part of the song:-

> *I will rest in your promises*
> *My confidence is your faithfulness*
> *I will rest in your promises*
> *My confidence is your faithfulness*

We then closed the service with my absolute favourite song *'Goodness of God'*.

I love You Lord
Oh Your mercy never fails me
All my days
I've been held in Your hands
From the moment that I wake up
Until I lay my head
I will sing of the goodness of God

All my life You have been faithful
All my life You have been so, so good
With every breath that I am able
I will sing of the goodness of God

I love Your voice
You have led me through the fire
In darkest nights
You are close like no other
I've known You as a father
I've known You as a friend
I have lived in the goodness of God

Your goodness is running after,
it's running after me
With my life laid down, I'm surrendered now, I
give you everything

As we sang this song, my two *'dancing sisters'*, Grace and Vivienne G, took to the floor, rejoicing and dancing. Even at this early stage of the journey, the above song had become my testimony. As each new day dawned, His goodness was literally chasing me down and I remember feeling overwhelmed as this was tangible. I have barely had time to stop and appreciate one mercy before the next one has overtaken me. The goodness and mercy of God are faster every time and I would never be able to outrun them.

According to the familiar Psalm, all my adversaries have witnessed the Lord prepare a table for me in the midst of my enemies:-

The Lord is my shepherd, I lack nothing.
He makes me lie down in green pastures,
he leads me beside quiet waters,
he refreshes my soul.
He guides me along the right paths
for his name's sake.
Even though I walk
through the darkest valley
I will fear no evil,
for you are with me;
your rod and your staff,
they comfort me. You prepare a
table before me
in the presence of my enemies.
You anoint my head with oil;
my cup overflows.
Surely your goodness and love will follow me
all the days of my life,
and I will dwell in the house of
the Lord forever.

(Psalm 23)

At times, my cup has overflowed and I have been used to minister to others. This has involved praying for the sick, supporting those struggling with addiction, supporting ex offenders and receiving words of knowledge for others.

Returning to the Sunday meeting – before leaving to come home, a sister came over to me and said that when Pastor Ron had been praying for me, the Holy Spirit had given her the following scripture:-

Blessed is she who has regard for the weak; the Lord delivers her in times of trouble. The Lord will protect her and preserve her life; He will bless her in the land and not surrender her to the desire of her foes. The Lord will sustain her on her sickbed and restore her from her bed of illness.
(Psalm 41 v 1-3)

The Holy Spirit had brought another word and this went a layer deeper given my heart for prisoners, ex offenders and the broken. From the beginning of this day, the Lord had clearly been speaking and moving and, once home, these words from the Lord were typed up, printed off and put on the wall in our front room.

That evening some of the leaders from another church I have been involved with over the years, paid a visit to our home and prayed, again in accordance with the scripture in James.

I Considered Not

Abraham once found himself with the odds stacked against him. Every carnal and human reason stood and sought to obstruct what God had said *was* coming to pass. Abraham did not deal in logic and neither did he waver or hover between two opinions. He did not negotiate or hold any self-consultations. He did not stagger through unbelief but stood firm on the promises of God.

On Tuesday 10th December, I had to undergo a neuropsychological evaluation to determine the pattern of brain-related strengths and weaknesses. This was somewhat amusing as many of my close friends and family will be aware that my general knowledge is very poor and this did not help with the assessment. Part of what the neuropsychologist does is to test your recognition of items. For example, she would show me a picture of a plant and ask what it was. I would reply: "*It's a plant*", there would then follow a pause and I would then be asked *"and can you tell me anymore? Do you know what sort of a plant this is?"* After this happened a few times, I think the neuropsychologist was getting the general feel of things. I did have to laugh and kept explaining that it was definitely a lack of general knowledge that was causing the problems of recognition.

Wednesday 11th December was a very heavy day consisting of a pre-surgical assessment followed by an appointment in the neurological department. For the medics, the procedures are just common day, but to be sat and be told in such a matter of fact way that you are going to have your head drilled through whilst being awake is somewhat hard to bear. This procedure was *going* to happen and, despite at first not wanting it, I eventually accepted that it was necessary. Even so, I did not wish to know the ins and outs and to be talked through in my hearing. If it needs doing, just get on with it and spare me the details.

As with any surgery, the medics walk you through the risks such as the possibility of dying and the risk of developing blood clots. I was sat down and told that during the procedure they would be running tests including putting volts through my brain to check they were not taking out essential tissue. They told me this surgery would require a long recovery time afterwards.

That next day, Pastor Andrew and Pastor Ron came to visit. It was very clear to them both that I was at complete peace and was overflowing with joy, both of which were miraculous. During our time together, Pastor Ron said that peace was to be my umpire through this season and that I would have an increased intimacy with Christ. I testify to this being the case throughout. I cannot go back to where I had been prior to this season. I was not in a bad place but the Bible speaks clearly about being either hot or cold. I had come to know Jesus in new ways and walked very closely, acutely tuned in to His voice and as I have sought after Him, I have found Him in new ways and He has started to reveal to me some of the secrets of His heart.

> *They asked each other, "Were not our hearts*
> *burning within us while he talked with us on*
> *the road and opened the Scriptures to us?"*
> *(Luke 24 v 32)*

The surgery (*an awake craniotomy plus a resection of a frontal lobe lesion*) was only offered on a Monday and the dates given were 16th or 23rd December. We were told that there was around 30% chance that this would be on 16th as someone was ahead of me on the list but their operation couldn't go ahead unless there was a bed for them in the ICU.

From the get go, I have been disinterested in regard to any of the medical information offered up, just knowing I had brain surgery whilst being awake. I have not read any of the leaflets, booklets or help cards the medics have passed to Pete. For me, it was simple. None of this was to be given any of my time or attention. The enemy is a liar. I have always known from the beginning that I was held and kept in and by the hand of God and He was carrying me *through.* (*Pete has taken care of all paperwork, alongside being the resident pharmacist, supplying the 'temporary, deemed necessary' cocktail of drugs*).

The Word of God clearly says:-

> *Finally, brothers and sisters, whatever is true,*
> *whatever is noble, whatever is right, whatever*
> *is pure, whatever is lovely, whatever is*
> *admirable—if anything is excellent or*
> *praiseworthy—think about such things.*
> *(Philippians 4 v 8)*

(*Our family friend, Sean, based within the neurological department, had said I can ask him anything I need to know for the interest of those reading and to enable people to understand the depths of what I have had to walk through.*)

The hospital had asked that we be ready and prepared on 16[th,] just in case we *were* called in. I remember not having been allowed to eat or drink anything at all, not even a sip of water, from 2am.

Fear, You Lost Your Hold

Early on, Pete printed off a scripture and stuck this on the wall alongside the ones I had been given:-

Rejoice in the Lord always. I will say it again: Rejoice! Let your gentleness be evident to all. The Lord is near. Do not be anxious about anything, but in every situation, by prayer and petition, with thanksgiving, present your requests to God. And the peace of God, which transcends all understanding, will guard your hearts and your minds in Christ Jesus.
(Phillipians 4 v 4-7)

On the afternoon of Saturday 14th December, Faith came round and we sang high praises to our God.

Praise the Lord!

Sing to the Lord a new song,
And His praise in the assembly of saints.

Let Israel rejoice in their Maker;
Let the children of Zion be joyful in their King.
Let them praise His name with the dance;
Let them sing praises to Him with the timbrel and harp.
For the Lord takes pleasure in His people;
He will beautify the humble with salvation.

Let the saints be joyful in glory;
Let them sing aloud on their beds.
Let the high praises of God be in their mouth,

And a two-edged sword in their hand,
To execute vengeance on the nations,
And punishments on the peoples;
To bind their kings with chains,
And their nobles with fetters of iron;
To execute on them the written judgment—
This honour have all His saints.

Praise the Lord!

(Psalm 149)

We boldly declared the scriptures on the wall and by the time we reached about the third time round, Faith paused over the above scripture and told me there was something I was anxious about. At which point, I broke down in her arms. The medics had said there was a risk of their procedure leading to a seizure during surgery in which I would be awake. They said if this happened then they would just pour water over my brain. This brought a real sense of fear as having now experienced two of these ordeals, this thought terrified me. Faith took authority over this fear and it left immediately. Hallelujah! We thanked the Lord there and then for a straightforward, seizure-free surgery.

Sunday 15th December, the day before surgery, Josh and his then partner called in to see me and I was able to send them on their way with a large bag of Christmas presents. That evening, we attended a music concert in town where Beth was playing double bass. As is customary at such events, my mum and I ended up crying with laughter. Reading this back is quite something: the fact that I was at such peace and was so joyful the night before open awake brain surgery can only be God's doing. A table in the presence of my enemies and me filled with the presence of God.

Those who live according to the flesh have their minds set on what the flesh desires; but those who live in accordance with the Spirit have their minds set on what the Spirit desires. The mind governed by the flesh is death, but the mind governed by the Spirit is life and peace. The mind governed by the flesh is hostile to God; it does not submit to God's law, nor can it do so. Those who are in the realm of the flesh cannot please God. You, however, are not in the realm of the flesh but are in the realm of the Spirit, if indeed the Spirit of God lives in you. And if anyone does not have the Spirit of Christ, they do not belong to Christ. But if Christ is in you, then even though your body is subject to death because of sin, the Spirit gives life because of righteousness. And if the Spirit of him who raised Jesus from the dead is living in you, he who raised Christ from the dead will also give life to your mortal bodies because of his Spirit who lives in you.

(Romans 8 v 5-11)

I arose on the morning of December 16th and Pete packed a bag for what would be *another* night away from home. I remember having been stood at the end of our bed praising and worshipping when Pete came in to say we had been called as a bed was available.

Upon arrival at the hospital, Pete and I had to sit around until mid-afternoon in a general waiting area. Throughout this time I was at complete peace and remember being up on my feet praising with my earphones. The last song I recall listening to before being called through was *'Jehovah is Your Name'*. This song talks about *My* God being a mighty warrior and being great in battle. Despite not having been allowed anything to eat or drink since 2am that morning, I did not experience even a hint of a headache or dehydration.

I had asked that Sean please come to theatre with me. He would have been only too willing but since he was our friend, senior management had understandably said they would only allow him as far as the anaesthetic room. I should stress that this was Sean's day off from work. Not having a clear sense of what time the surgery would commence, he waited in the hospital from late morning until the surgery.

Late in the afternoon, Sean rejoined us in the little room in which I was waiting for theatre. This room was darkened and I was given a photosensitive dye to drink which meant that I would have to be kept in darkness for twenty-four hours. Prior to surgery, all lights along the way to the toilet were switched off for my own protection. The anaesthetist and surgeon came to visit followed shortly by a nurse with a gown and red socks. This time was somewhat strained, with me sat waiting whilst Pete and Sean were left trying to make conversation – which they did well. Finally, after an all-day wait, the moment arrived. Leaving Pete behind, but with my very own '*superhero*' at my side (another gift of grace), I was escorted on foot to the anaesthetic room.

At 4:30pm, I was greeted once again by the anaesthetist who had now been joined by a second one who was equally as kind. I received these men as servants God had handpicked. I remember Sean having to assist with my gown and then followed "sats probes", blood pressure cuffs, ECG dots and the cannulas. The anaesthetist struggled to get a cannula into my hand; never a pleasant experience. Seeing this was becoming somewhat of a battle for them and having to bang my hand hard to make any progress, Sean offered me his hand to hold.

At 4:45pm I was wheeled into theatre. Minus Sean now, I had a whole host of professionals awaiting my arrival. Sean has since informed me that this team comprised two anaesthetists, an anaesthetist practitioner, two surgeons, three scrub team, a neuropsychologist and a neuro-monitoring person. Now with my arrival, numbers stood at ten. Angels also surrounded each of these men and women permitted by God to work on me, so it was a very full, peaceful room with everyone divinely and strategically positioned.

I was conscious for the whole of the procedure and was positioned on the bed somewhere between lying down and sitting up, with the clock straight across from me. The neuropsychologist stood to my left the entire time, getting me to move my left hand and foot throughout. I was occasionally offered a sponge with water to moisten my mouth which I then caught on to and kept asking for. I also recall regularly trying to scratch my face; I had been warned a side effect of the dye could lead to itching on my face and I remember asking the neuropsychologist to please scratch my face for me. She was very reassuring through the whole thing and kept telling me how well I was doing.

The only point at which I remember feeling a little woozy was after they had put a local anaesthetic in my head before drilling a hole through my skull. True to their word, I did not feel any pain at all, although the drilling sensation was bizarre. *(It did take a while for me to return to using an electric toothbrush post-surgery because I linked the sound and sensation but recovery time was remarkably quick).*

Through many dangers, toils and snares
We have already come
T'was Grace that brought us safe thus far
And Grace will lead us home

Salt & Vinegar Crisps

I remember leaving theatre at 7pm having shouted out *"Thank you everyone!"* and then being wheeled through to the recovery suite. Though I had been given intravenous morphine in theatre, the young male nurse informed me that paracetamol by way of the drip was all that was on offer for now and proceeded to sort this. I was shortly offered a cup of tea and really fancied this but knowing that I was close to bed time, would not risk the caffeine keeping me awake. As it turned out I could have indulged – sleep was not on the agenda (I was in hospital after all). Cravings for salt and vinegar crisps kicked in and this might have been something to do with me remembering that Pete had some on him earlier in the day.

The nurse in charge of my care offered me biscuits, which I declined, insisting he please find me some salt and vinegar crisps. Whilst seeking to humour me, he continued to explain that as much as he could if he would, he had no way of acquiring crisps of any flavour. He proceeded to entice me with a selection of chocolate bourbons, custard creams and ginger biscuits. I eventually agreed to him bringing me '*lots of*' custard creams and ginger biscuits but insisted I did not want to catch sight of a bourbon...really not fancying these.

For the next couple of hours, I was kept company by my biscuit supplier and then when it was time for the *'never popular handover'*, he wished me all the best and I was then looked after by a lovely nurse who it turned out, lived near me.

The evening rolled on and despite having been deemed suitable for a move out of recovery some hours earlier, I found myself sat pretty much bolt upright waiting for a single room to become available, since I had to be kept in darkness.

Pete had been phoned by the recovery unit to say I was safely through the surgery and was doing well, but was not allowed to enter that area. By the grace of God, when clearly things were not progressing in terms of moving me on, I negotiated with the nurse to *please* allow him through. At approximately 9pm, we were reunited. It was not until 10pm that I was transferred up to my own room within the neuro ward. After a while, and having sought to settle me as much as he could, Pete and I said goodnight and Pete then returned home. (Pete had eaten the crisps earlier in the evening...)

Humbled, Not Degraded

This night was extremely challenging. Due to the type of surgery I had undergone, I was not allowed to lie down. Nurses did observations every half an hour, taking my pulse, blood pressure and shining lights in my eyes. Despite it being winter time, I kept the window open but still remember feeling hot and requesting cold compresses, drinks of water and a fan. Despite the nurses visiting every half an hour anyway, I remember calling them in regardless in between these times, feeling so frustrated and fed up.

Eventually, after what seemed like forever, morning did arrive, though I was kept in darkness due to effects of the dye. I was eventually given oral morphine but literally, within minutes of having taken this along with all the other meds I had been prescribed, I was violently sick; my body could not tolerate the morphine and from this point forward, paracetamol was all I took for pain relief. Having given birth without even any gas and air all those years back, this would be fine as my pain threshold is pretty high. I recall becoming very upset as I had literally thrown up all down the gown. Time for the buzzer again, and a kind nurse entered the room to find me sobbing suffering from exhaustion having not slept. I had had enough now and just wanted to go home. After gowning herself up, she helped me up off the bed. Being far too weak to leave the room for the toilet, which would have also involved all corridor lights having to be put off, I was assisted onto a commode and had to use this with the nurse stood close by. I remember feeling completely degraded especially when the nurse had to wash me as I was covered in vomit. Later on I realised the word I needed to use was '*humbled*'. As pleasant as this nurse was, I longed for Pete to be there to help.

Shortly after I was sorted out with a new gown and back in the bed, when Pete arrived. I was once again upset as I had been missed for the breakfast call so had not even had a cup of tea. Pete was on the case and shortly after arrived tea and toast; better late than never.

The rest of this day remains a bit of a blur but consisted of a lot of waiting around in a hot dark room. Late morning, and I was collected for another scan. Just when I thought things could not become even more humiliating, I had to wear a gown, red socks, surgical stockings and to top it all, a blindfold due to having to be kept in the dark. I was then wheeled through the corridors, backwards into a lift and to the scanner.

Pete later informed me that he had seen at least three people we knew that day whilst he had gone to get us both drinks and food. Imagine they had seen me!

The motion of the lift was most unpleasant and once in the scanner room, I was completely dependent on the two nurses to help me out of the wheelchair and into the scanner and then the reverse. They were lovely and having discovered I had been left with ECG dots on my chest, removed these prior to entering the scanner.

Perfect Timing

Whilst I had been whisked away to the scanner, Pete informed me that a *'cancer nurse'* had attempted to come and talk with me and would call back later. I politely knocked back an offer of a return visit as I had no interest or reason to be entertaining conversation with her. What awesome timing.

As the day went on, I longed for light and at around 4pm, my wish was granted. After being asked numerous times questions like, *"Do you know where you are?"* and *"Do you know who the prime minister is?"* I was deemed safe to return home. Occupational health also visited to see if I was sufficiently mobile and thankfully the decision was a positive one. However, we now had to wait for the pharmacist... only a bit longer and then we were free to leave the oppressive environment.

(We had two phone calls from occupational health once home requesting they to come out to assess me;

these appointments were not required; I was running up and down the stairs).

Finally, the pharmacist called by and Pete headed off to locate a wheelchair to get me to the car.

My mum was at home with Beth and Anna. I remember being shattered but knowing I needed to eat something. Before heading back to the other side of town to collect medication, Pete prepared me a small baked potato as I really fancied one and I then gently '*hit*' the pillow as I was now allowed to lie down as normal. This was a strange experience as I could sense a real tightness where they had sliced me open and stapled me back together again. I had a cough at this time and every time I coughed, would brace myself as it would feel like the staples were going to pull apart. I slept on just my left hand side for at least a week before being confident and vaguely comfortable to attempt to try lying on my right side due to the positioning of the scar. This scar will always speak to me of the love, grace and mercy of Jesus; a constant reminder of His goodness. It will always tell a story and the ripples will travel far and wide resulting in the extension of the Kingdom.

Every Verse, My Story

On the evening of 19th December, Pete and I were sat on our bed desperately trying to get on the unfortunately necessary surgical stockings - thankfully only a two week post-surgery requirement. I remember commenting that one day soon, we would look back at this episode and laugh.

Just then, the Holy Spirit brought to mind a scripture I knew existed somewhere, most likely in the Psalms. It was about *advancing against a troop and leaping over a wall.* I asked Pete if he knew where it was in the Bible but he was unsure.

I thought nothing more about this and then had, what counted at that time, as a great night sleep, sleeping from 10pm till 2am. At around 2.30am, I had a very real sense in my spirit that people were praying for me.

When I checked my messages, I had one from my sister, Faith. She said she had been awake and praying for people that needed sleep in the early hours of that morning. She then went on to say:-

"I just see you climbing over every hurdle; every setback; every bit of junk the devil foolishly throws at you!"

She then signed off:-

"Lots of love...Psalm 18".

Upon looking up Psalm 18, I was amazed to find it completely summed up the experience I was walking through! Then I read:-

For by You I can run against a troop,
By my God I can leap over a wall.
(Psalm 18 v 29)

The Holy Spirit had given me just one verse of this Psalm the previous night and then Faith had then sent this *very* scripture through. I love it when God confirms His Word.

Praise and worship music was a constant in the early days of this season and pretty much throughout. Pete bought a Chromecast to enable me to watch preaching and praise and worship on the TV – allowing the atmosphere of our home to be filled to capacity with Truth. My mum and myself listened to many hours of powerful preaching, and again, two of the first messages we listened to were based around Psalm 18; I had not even searched for 'Psalm 18', I was simply looking for preaching around the subject of faith.

I love you, Lord, my strength.

The Lord is my rock, my fortress
and my deliverer;
my God is my rock, in whom I take refuge,
my shield and the horn of my salvation, my
stronghold.

I called to the Lord, who is worthy of praise,
and I have been saved from my enemies.

(Psalm 18 v 1-3)

Psalm 18 is my story. The first part of the Psalm is a declaration of who God is. God was not only my God, but My Father too and so I started making bold declarations over my life. These declarations and confessions were coming from a place of confidence. As God was my Father and I was His child, I knew He had responsibilities and charges over me. There was a covenant between me and Him that *He* had established. A contract can be broken, simply if one party fails to keep their promise. A covenant, however, puts no conditions on faithfulness. A contract is signed but can be revoked; contract terms can be changed, but a covenant is sealed. The covenant I am talking about is not just an ordinary covenant. This covenant was sealed once and for all with the precious blood of Jesus. The Godhead, Father, Son and Holy Spirit all involved. I knew who My God was and as a result, knew who I was as His child. I was boldly declaring the infallible Word of God.

My Strength; any strength I could potentially seek to muster up to face this *giant* down in the valley, was never going to be sufficient; it was going to have to be all *His* strength and this was going to have to be a daily supply.

My Rock; He was a sure and certain foundation, remaining fastened on this Rock meant I was immovable and steadfast. God had spoken and what He had spoken was to come to pass.

I went on and declared Him to be My Fortress, My Deliverer, My Shield, My Stronghold; my only place of safety, perfectly protected from every fiery dart the enemy had designed and had lined up for me; my only defence from all danger and a place not susceptible to outside influences or disturbances.

I boldly declared that Jesus secured the necessary victory for me over 2000 years ago when he laid down His life so that I might live abundant life. Death could not hold Him down and consequently the resurrection power that raised Him from the dead was living and working in me and this power could not be withstood!

I had called upon the Lord and He was saving me from every enemy. I was wall to wall surrounded, every brick a scripture. He had heard my cry and had responded. He did not send an angel but came Himself. God hates my enemies more than I do and was waiting for an opportunity to show Himself strong on my behalf.

Good Tidings

A week after surgery, on Christmas Eve, we had an appointment with a consultant supported by a specialist nurse. They announced over me a most aggressive form of brain tumour and then went on to explain that this sort likes to '*invade*'. Upon hearing these words something happened in my spirit and I remember laughing out loud. I had the mind of Christ (*according to 1 Corinthians 2 v 16*) and I immediately silenced this lying voice in the Mighty Name of Jesus. The only '*invasion*' this temple would be experiencing would be that of the Holy Spirit of God.

Now temporarily under the care of the oncology department, I was starting to hear statements like:- "*Now you are a cancer patient...*", and being told about "*Your tumour*". Every word spoken over me by anyone other than God that did not line up with the Word and report of the Lord, I took authority over in the Name of Jesus and rendered those words null and void. The devil is a liar.

The medics apologised to have to '*break the news*' on Christmas Eve but I can honestly say that despite their announcement being based on medical facts and carnal knowledge, it did not move me at all. Psalm 18 all the way... Stepping into the hospital was simply like stepping into the world's viewpoint on the situation but the voice of Jesus was the only voice I was listening to. The fact that it was Christmas Eve, only caused me to rejoice more.

*But the angel said to them, "Do not be afraid.
I bring you good news that will cause great
joy for all the people. Today in the town of
David a Saviour has been born to you; he is
the Messiah, the Lord.   This will be a sign to
you: You will find a baby wrapped in cloths
and lying in a manger."
Suddenly a great company of the heavenly
host appeared with the angel,
praising God and saying,
"Glory to God in the highest heaven,
and on earth peace to those on
whom his favour rests."
(Luke 2 v 10-14)*

I remember thinking my lack of response or failure to burst into tears could possibly cause them to believe I was in denial. All I knew was that this giant was coming down and this was God's battle. He was greater, stronger, higher than any other, my Healer and awesome in power. The medics' '*findings*' were nothing more than a footnote. The glory that was to come out from this situation far outweighed any lie or scheme of the enemy and he was to regret the moment he asked God for permission to touch me.

*I consider that our present sufferings are not
worth comparing with the glory that will be
revealed in us. For the creation waits in eager
expectation for the children of
God to be revealed.
(Romans 8 v 18-19)*

I was fully convinced that this situation was all for the purpose set out in the scripture above and no plan of the enemy would in any way succeed.

Before being allowed to head home that afternoon, we then went through to another room where I sat on the side of a bed gritting my teeth whilst the nurse removed the staples from my head; no pain relief on offer. The surgery had only been a week ago, so this area was still very tender. However, she seemed confident she knew what she was doing, despite it feeling like she had taken to a classroom notice board with a staple remover, pushing the implement she was using up under each and every staple.

Bring out the 'Johnsons'

After having had the staples removed, I was told I was now allowed to wash my hair, however, I did not like touching my head in case I hurt it; the area where they sliced and drilled was very tight and sensitive. Johnsons baby shampoo, conditioner and a soft bristled baby brush at the ready, a first attempt was made. I was only allowed to stand in the shower for this and not lean over a basin. I recall being so nervous and even after a couple of washes every couple of days, there still remained a fair amount of dried blood that I had not been brave enough to deal with. This simply looked like purple hair dye. Eventually, with Pete's encouragement, I managed to finally resolve this.

The week after I had had surgery, one of the young men we had live with us, called in to collect his

Christmas presents. My hair must have looked a complete state especially given what I have mentioned above. As usual, he gave me a big hug, bless him, and handed me a huge bouquet of flowers and chocolates. He apologised for not having wrapped them for me for Christmas but had stopped at the shop on his way over with his girlfriend. This meant so much to me. Before he left, I showed him my hair and he seriously had not even noticed! After having him live with us for a year, I knew he was telling the truth. Funny memories...

A Divine Download

On the morning of Monday 30th December, I had a visit from Beki. We spent a wonderful time together talking about the goodness of God. Upon reading the scriptures on the wall, I remember Beki laughing at the mention of an *'apparent sickbed'* in the Lamentations word. I had not spent any time other than night times in bed, had never needed to take a rest during the day and can testify to not ever feeling tired.

Before leaving, Beki said we would pray and she knelt at my feet on the floor with her bible open at Psalm 18. Beki was hearing directly from the Father-heart and started by telling me that My Father was pleased with me and thanked me for trusting and believing in Him as I could have chosen not to. She said He was carrying me on His shoulders and said that there was an *untangling* going on:-

The cords of death entangled me;
the torrents of destruction overwhelmed me.
The cords of the grave coiled around me;
the snares of death confronted me.
(Psalm 18 v 4-5)
He reached down from on high and
took hold of me;
he drew me out of deep waters.
(Psalm 18 v 16)

Beki went on to say that she had seen God's hand reaching down and lifting me out of the waters and had said that as He lifted me out, many others were holding on to my legs and feet. As they held on to me, they too were pulled out of the water and also some were pulled out of a much stickier tar-like substance.

> *He rescued me from my powerful enemy,*
> *from my foes, who were too strong for me.*
> *(Psalm 18 v 17)*

Beki went on to say that I would be helping people who hate themselves or have never been loved properly so are numb to being loved. She had seen people whose nerve endings had been burned resulting in a compelling fear of trusting others, since trust had always resulted in hurt.

> *The Lord has dealt with me according*
> *to my righteousness;*
> *according to the cleanness of my hands he*
> *has rewarded me.*
> *(Psalm 18 v 20)*

Finally, she said that anyone I help can also step into the righteousness and forgiveness of Jesus, becoming completely new and clean.

Once Beki had left, I had to attend the Princess Anne Hospital for a mammogram. The medics were being very thorough with no area unsearched. After a short wait, I was taken through and informed that, straight after this procedure, I would be called through for a follow up ultra sound, just to be extra vigilant. I was surprised to hear this as we had not been informed of this ahead of the appointment.

After the mammogram, I returned to the waiting area. The nurse then returned and informed me that the results of the mammogram indicated no need for any further investigations and we were free to return home.

My faith-filled sister Rita, a fellow Sycamore Tree volunteer, shared the following with me on 11th February, another reference to rising from waters.

> *"I will rise from waters deep*
> *Into the saving arms of God*
> *And I will sing salvation songs*
> *Jesus Christ has set me free"*

Signed & Sealed in Blood

On Sunday 29th December, Pastor Andrew was talking about having a vision for 2020. He reminded us that the Father had a purpose and a destiny for each of our lives and talked about the importance of speaking about days to come. He said God wanted to use us to see broken lives restored and so we were encouraged to speak the language of heaven.

Early in the meeting he said he felt a mantle of authority come on him. He said that we were going to break the power of the enemy in someone's life. I was then called out and authority was taken over everything that was trying to come against my body. He then went on to thank the Lord for every trace of cancer having gone in Jesus Name and thanked Him for the faith that had been deposited within me. He declared 2020 would be a year of health for me and went on to prophesy long life, declaring that I was going see both my daughters marry, become a grandmother, a great grandmother and an old lady declaring the goodness of God. He declared this sickness was *not unto death* in Jesus Name. Pastor Ron and Pastor Josh then continued to minister. Pastor Josh decreed and declared:- *"Fi; It is well with you!"*

This time was not rushed and the Holy Spirit was given time to move without restriction. We would continue to believe '*the report of the Lord'*.

We then sang out the old song:-

"It is well
With my soul
It is well, it is well with my soul".

On New Year's Eve we celebrated together at church. I could not remain in my seat and went to the front to dance alongside my brothers Ace and Lloyd. We sang:-

"Who has the final say?
Jehovah has the final say
Jehovah turns my life around
Jehovah turns my life around
He makes a way where there is no way
Jehovah has the final say"

I danced and declared that Jehovah Rapha had the final say over my life, that He *had* turned my life around and that He *had* made a way where there was no way. We now waited for what had happened in the spiritual realm to manifest in the physical realm.

It was prophesied early on, that my head would be the talk of the hospital and as you will see through this book, this has been the case.

Fight the Good Fight of Faith

Faith does not operate in the realm of the possible. There is no glory for God in that which is humanly possible. Faith is not an emotion; it is a decision and God honours faith. However, faith and fear *cannot* reside together.

> *For whatever is born of God overcomes the world. And this is the victory that has overcome the world, our faith.*
> *(1 John 5 v 4)*

No sickness seeking to come against my body was from God; it was straight from the very pit of hell itself. God's will is that I walk in divine health and enjoy abundant life. I was standing firm on the promises of God and knew He would fulfil His Word to me.

> *The end of a matter is better*
> *than its beginning;*
> *patience is better than pride.*
> *(Ecclesiastes 7 v 8)*

1st January 2020 Pastor Dennis called for a catch up. I remember saying to him that to God, there was no difference whatsoever between cancer and a common cold and we rejoiced together over this.

> *As Jesus went on from there, two blind men*
> *followed him, calling out, "Have mercy on us,*
> *Son of David!" When he had gone indoors,*
> *the blind men came to him, and he asked*
> *them, "Do you believe that I am able to do*

this?" "Yes, Lord," they replied. Then he touched their eyes and said, "According to your faith let it be done to you"; and their sight was restored.
(Matthew 9 v 27-29)

Following our phone call, he then sent me the message below:-

"The one thing that brings the favour of God into a situation or circumstance that a disciple of Jesus is in, is belief in God's Word! Believing the Word attracts the favour of God. The woman with the issue of blood said "I know if I can just touch the hem of his garment, I know I will be healed". She went down on her knees and came from behind and touched the end of the tassel on His garment, which was white and spoke of His righteousness, and a blue chord running through it, speaking of the covenant He made with His people, and the 613 knots, which spoke of His precepts and promises in the covenant contract! She went to Jesus, the Word and pulled on His righteous covenant and suddenly virtue flowed out of the Word and healed her. The same power of virtue was flowing as you were speaking to me on the phone. I could hear faith in action as you were reciting what the Word says, to me! Love and blessings..."

It was faith that would allow the power of God to work in me as this battle was fought. The enemy of my soul was going to constantly be seeking to weaken my faith by means of threats and intimidation whilst trying to convince me to listen to his lies.

Submit yourselves, then, to God. Resist the devil, and he will flee from you.
(James 4 v 7)

Take note who resists and who does the fleeing.

Be alert and of sober mind. Your enemy the devil prowls around like a roaring lion looking for someone to devour. Resist him, standing firm in the faith, because you know that the family of believers throughout the world is undergoing the same kind of sufferings. And the God of all grace, who called you to his eternal glory in Christ, after you have suffered a little while, will himself restore you and make you strong, firm and steadfast. To him be the power forever and ever. Amen."
(1 Peter 5 v 8-11)

Our warfare is to be aggressive, *not* passive. We should not be sitting waiting for the enemy to attack so we can resist him. He should be given no time to breathe. We should be carrying the battle to him and his gates shall not withstand our assault. Even the devils believe and tremble. We should be bringing fear and trembling to the enemy rather than constantly worrying about when he will next attack us.

For though we live in the world, we do not wage war as the world does. The weapons we fight with are not the weapons of the world. On the contrary, they have divine power to demolish strongholds. We demolish arguments and every pretension that sets

itself up against the knowledge of God, and we take captive every thought to make it obedient to Christ. And we will be ready to punish every act of disobedience, once your obedience is complete.
(2 Corinthians 10 v 3-6)

These weapons *are* mighty but not if we sit and wait for the enemy to attack us. Weapons stored in an arsenal have no effect; it is only as and when we use them that we find them to be powerful and sharper than any two-edged sword. We are called to bring destruction and demolition to the enemy's empire. We are called to be soldiers fully clothed in His armour.

Finally, be strong in the Lord and in his mighty power. Put on the full armour of God, so that you can take your stand against the devil's schemes. For our struggle is not against flesh and blood, but against the rulers, against the authorities, against the powers of this dark world and against the spiritual forces of evil in the heavenly realms. Therefore put on the full armour of God, so that when the day of evil comes, you may be able to stand your ground, and after you have done everything, to stand. Stand firm then, with the belt of truth buckled around your waist, with the breastplate of righteousness in place, and with your feet fitted with the readiness that comes from the gospel of peace. In addition to all this, take up the shield of faith, with which you can extinguish all the flaming arrows of the evil one. Take the helmet of salvation and the sword of the Spirit, which is the word of God.

And pray in the Spirit on all occasions with all kinds of prayers and requests. With this in mind, be alert and always keep on praying for all the Lord's people.

(Ephesians 6 v 10-18)

Throughout this season I had taken to me the full armour of God. By the grace of God, I have done what verse 16 has said to do. I have taken up my *shield of faith* and with this *shield of faith,* I have extinguished every fiery dart, in Jesus' Name.

Return to Sender

When the Lord restored the fortunes of Zion,
we were like those who dreamed.
Our mouths were filled with laughter,
our tongues with songs of joy.
Then it was said among the nations,
"The Lord has done great things for them."
The Lord has done great things for us,
and we are filled with joy.

Restore our fortunes, Lord,
like streams in the Negev.
Those who sow with tears
will reap with songs of joy.
Those who go out weeping,
carrying seed to sow,
will return with songs of joy,
carrying sheaves with them.
(Psalm 126)

Very early in 2020, it was prophesied that my family and I are made for signs and wonders.

Here am I, and the children the Lord has
given me. We are signs and symbols in Israel
from the Lord Almighty, who dwells on
Mount Zion.
(Isaiah 8 v 18)

Faith and I made it more than plain to the kingdom of darkness that we were unsure who the enemy was looking for but they sure did not live here! We declared to every principality and power *'Not known at this address!'* and *'return to sender!'*

The item sent had become *'undeliverable'* as I had never taken ownership of any of it. Never signed for it! We *'boomeranged'* it back to the pit of hell and declared a backfiring upon the kingdom of darkness.

That same afternoon, Faith received revelation from the Holy Spirit regarding *'the oil having found a container'*; like in 2 Kings 4; I was to find as many vessels as I could and keep pouring the oil. This would overflow and affect many lives. This pouring out of the oil was starting to happen throughout the process with me ministering to others and this included me praying for the sick and seeing them recover.

Faith then declared:-

"The Lord has done great things for Fi!"

We do not want you to be uninformed, brothers and sisters, about the troubles we experienced in the province of Asia. We were under great pressure, far beyond our ability to endure, so that we despaired of life itself. Indeed, we felt we had received the sentence of death. But this happened that we might not rely on ourselves but on God, who raises the dead. He has delivered us from such a deadly peril, and he will deliver us again. On him we have set our hope that he will continue to deliver us, as you help us by your prayers. Then many will give thanks on our behalf for

***the gracious favour granted us in answer to
the prayers of many.
(2 Corinthians 1 v 8-11)***

Faith and I have never sat and done small talk and I can count on one hand the numbers of cups of tea we have shared over the years. This afternoon was no different; there was territory to be fought for and taken. The thief had been found and exposed, attempting to kill me and take me out the game as he had some understanding of what God had prepared for me to do in terms of His Kingdom being extended.

***For it is by grace you have been saved,
through faith—and this is not from
yourselves, it is the gift of God, not by works,
so that no one can boast. For we are God's
handiwork, created in Christ Jesus to do good
works, which God prepared in advance
for us to do.
(Ephesians 2 v 8-10)***

It was going to be glorious and there was no way the enemy wanted me to enter into all that God had planned for me; he would contend every step of the way. I was not prepared to settle this side of the Jordan, the Lord had brought me this far and He was taking me the whole way in. Faith and I declared this assignment cancelled in Jesus' Mighty Name.

The enemy had not only tried to kill me, he had also attempted to steal. My paid employment as a support worker is an on-the-road job and requires me to drive. I was taken from behind the wheel for a season, due to legal requirements, but we laugh at this temporary constraint because what comes out of all this is not going to be worth comparing. My brother Steven said the Holy Spirit had shown him very clearly that God's future plan for me involved my own set of car keys and a Bible.

The enemy made another wrong assumption. He figured that with the treatment the medics would deem necessary for me I would no longer be able to tutor in the prison as I would have no way of getting there and, even if I could secure a regular lift, I would not be well enough due to the side effects of medication. What a pack of nonsense! I had a lift to prison every week, stood on my feet and tutored every session and suffered not one side effect from chemotherapy.

Mondays @ 1pm

The day I met with Beki back in December, she mentioned there were a couple of other '*faith filled*' ladies that she was close to in her church. One of these ladies was Catherine. I knew *of* her as we had met briefly a couple of years back to discuss something on her heart in relation to prison but we had not spoken since.

Monday 6th January, was the start of a new season; a very significant period of time for both myself and Catherine. Mondays at 1pm were going to become something special, you could just feel it.

I told Catherine that I was coming through this experience with '*fire in my belly*' all for the glory of God. I remember her saying that she also believed this and that I would be coming out of this '*roaring*'!

One of the first Mondays we met, Catherine felt to give me the following scripture and her words were:-

'Fi - This is your mandate! To set the prisoners free'

The Spirit of the Sovereign Lord is on me,
because the Lord has anointed me
to proclaim good news to the poor.
He has sent me to bind up the broken hearted,
to proclaim freedom for the captives
and release from darkness for the prisoners.
(Isaiah 61 v 1)

I had a destiny and this was to be contended for. The enemy's kingdom was under certain threat and devastation and the freedom of many was at stake.

One time we met, the presence of the Holy Spirit was so tangible and I remember Catherine commenting that she could feel the fire of God when we prayed together and she could see my face literally blazing with holy fire!

Catherine saw me in the spirit clothed in golden robes, wearing a crown of beautiful jewels and holding a golden sceptre and a large sword.

> *I will clothe his enemies with shame,*
> *but his head will be adorned with a radiant*
> *crown.*
> *(Psalm 132 v 18)*

Catherine told me that the Father was proud of me and *I* was beginning to catch His heart for me and also for those I knew He had lined up for me to connect with. Not only was my Father my *'Dad'* and had a heart filled with compassion and mercy for me, he was *also* God Almighty and had something to say about the state of affairs I was currently walking through. Nothing had caught Him by surprise and He was walking the journey with me, His presence continually within, above, before, behind, below and around me.

> *Where can I go from your Spirit?*
> *Where can I flee from your presence?*
> *If I go up to the heavens, you are there;*
> *if I make my bed in the depths, you are there.*

If I rise on the wings of the dawn,
if I settle on the far side of the sea,
even there your hand will guide me,
your right hand will hold me fast.
If I say, "Surely the darkness will hide me
and the light become night around me,"
even the darkness will not be dark to you;
the night will shine like the day,
for darkness is as light to you.
(Psalm 139:7-12)

Catherine said the Holy Spirit had shown her very clearly that I was in an ark, similar to the one Noah was in when the floods were upon the earth. Within this ark, I was completely covered and not a drop of water could penetrate. I would be aware of things going on peripherally but that was the limit. The gale force winds *would* blow, causing the ark to rock harshly from side to side; I *would* hear the thunders roar, the oceans *would* rise; there *would* be a sudden and occasional passing through of some choppy waters. However, the height of the waves or the strength of the wind would make *no* difference whatsoever to *my* stance within the ark. My Father was also King reigning and ruling over this storm. Within the ark, I was completely covered; weatherproof and *'negative'* proof!

Another way to explain the way God was allowing me to walk though this season would be like saying I was out walking on a very cold day, having heard the weather report and knowing the *'facts'*, but wearing a thick warm coat with a cosy scarf and hat and therefore not feeling the cold. Knowing it *was* cold but not being affected by the temperature, due to being suitably prepared for the occasion.

Back to the ark, the occurrences that I would be aware of would present themselves in different guises. These could be negative words of hopelessness spoken over me by others including the medical profession, experts in their fields, or other Christians not understanding my stance and seeking to challenge my *immovable* position. Some could speak of me being in apparent 'denial' and thinking me mad to not consider what I was up against in the natural; some Christians did not really know how to respond to such strong faith (a gift I believe God has given me not only for myself to travel through this season, but as according to the scripture, for the building up of the whole of the Body):-

There are different kinds of gifts, but the same Spirit distributes them. There are different kinds of service, but the same Lord. There are different kinds of working, but in all of them and in everyone it is the same God at work.

Now to each one the manifestation of the Spirit is given for the common good. To one there is given through the Spirit a message of wisdom, to another a message of knowledge by means of the same Spirit, to another faith by the same Spirit, to another gifts of healing by that one Spirit, to another miraculous powers, to another prophecy, to another distinguishing between spirits, to another speaking in different kinds of tongues, and to still another the interpretation of tongues. All these are the work of one and the same Spirit, and he distributes them to each one, just as he determines.

(1 Corinthians 12 v 4-11)

On the 10th February, we had the most wonderful, gentle time of worship. The wind outside had dropped and the birds literally joined in with their chorus. I had never experienced this before but Catherine said that this had been her experience many a time when worshipping. Catherine was playing beautifully on the piano and I caught what I can best describe as a vision from the Lord of me in an ark, coming into land. I was not far from shore and when I reached the dry ground, I remember seeing mountains ahead. I took the covering off the ark and pulled myself out, my left leg, followed by my right leg. I was clothed in hessian trousers and a white top. I had clearly been *through* an experience; a storm; but had finally reached the desired destination. As I climbed out onto literal dry land, the storm having passed, I realised that this was a thirsty land, full of people desperately waiting for help; I had landed on assignment.

With tears of joy gently rolling down my cheeks, I shared this vision with Catherine and we rejoiced together. Within a couple of minutes of her having left our home, the Holy Spirit gave me a song. This was not a song I had sang for a very long time and was such a wonderful confirmation of what had just happened! The song was entitled '*Holy Moment*' and some of the lyrics say:-

"This is a Holy moment
Come with expectation
Everything abandoned
Look and see the Glory of our God
Lift your voice to heaven
Jesus is our anthem
Celebrate the wonder of His love

He is here with us now

For your honour and fame
Fall again in this place
Fill us up as we overflow with praise."

The last time we met prior to lockdown[2] was so precious and timely. As we were praying, the Holy Spirit confirmed we were close to the finishing line. Catherine heard in the spirit realm, the words:-*"You chose life!"*

He asked you for life, and you
gave it to him—
length of days, forever and ever.
(Psalm 21 v 4)

Catherine could hear the sound of heaven applauding me; a sound of being cheered on by a '*great cloud of witnesses*'. I have always said I would be running

---

[2] In 2020 the UK and most of the world was subjected to a period of "lockdown" where people were confined to their houses to prevent the spread of COVID19.

over the finish line of this trial, full pelt. I have been inspired by Godly examples of many that have gone before, including my dad. Death did not find agreement with me and the trial was over. It was now just a case of walking it out. We thanked the Lord for the completion and wholeness that is going to be made manifest.

Catherine writes:-

"I first met Fi a couple of years ago, when I asked her if we could meet up, to talk about a vision I had received from the Lord. The vision was about me going into a prison and singing the love of the Father over the prisoners. In the vision, I saw men weeping as their hearts were being melted and lives being turned around as a result of an encounter with the Father's love.

We met on Friday 19th January 2018 and chatted over coffee. Fi told me that she could not see a way for this vision to become a reality at that time, given the situation in the prison she was connected to. But, what I did not know, was that God was opening another door which we did not walk through until the beginning of 2020.

I had seen on our church Facebook page, that Fi had been rushed into hospital and had been given a serious diagnosis; I had felt led to pray for her. Following surgery she contacted me and asked if I would come and visit her, knowing that I was also a woman of great faith. I immediately said yes and went to see her on Monday 6th January.

When I arrived on her doorstep, she greeted me with such a happy glowing face; I knew that this was not going to be a typical meet up. As she brought me into her front room, I could see bible verses up on the wall speaking life and words of prophecy about her future. She began straight away to tell me everything that had happened to her regarding her health and the diagnosis and how it all seemed connected to her ministry. She told me about how something significant was happening in the area of ministry when suddenly from nowhere she was taken into hospital, having had a seizure whilst driving!

God had been using Fi and her family, to help and support vulnerable young people and this seemed like some kind of spiritual attack to try and stop this from happening. I was struck by how matter of fact she was and did not show any sign of being emotional, despairing or fearful. Fi told me that she knew God was with her and that the diagnosis was only a temporary season that she was to walk through and that she would come out completely healed and restored. I was overwhelmed by her unwavering faith and how single minded she was.

Dying was not a possibility as she knew without a shadow of a doubt that this was not her time and refused to give any consideration to any reports from the medics. She would not even read the letters that they had sent out stating all their facts because the only words she would allow herself to see were God's words of life from scripture and there was not any mention of death in there! I was

122

totally blown away by this and marveled at her attitude in the worst of circumstances you could be given.

We started to pray together every Monday and as the Holy Spirit came, I was able to pray boldly for her, already sensing that God had already answered our prayers. Mondays had now become a weekly event and I always felt so uplifted and encouraged by all the testimonies Fi was telling me about as she still continued to go into the prison to run the course she was doing with the men there. Her energy and enthusiasm continued and never once did I ever see her lose heart or even look tired!

Many people had been praying for Fi as she started chemo and radiotherapy. We all prayed that there would be no ill side effects but only healing and good.

After a few weeks of praying together, I suggested going into her conservatory and doing some worship together as there was a piano. Our times of worship were beautiful and week by week, we encountered a greater measure of the Holy Spirit and were able to pray with much more authority and boldness.

There was one week that we both remember fondly, when after singing, I began to just play very lightly on the piano and the peace of God filled the room. We could hear the birds singing so loudly and sweetly and the wind dropped. During this moment

Fi saw a vision of herself in an ark and it was coming into rest!

Every Monday became something we both looked forward to. We always left each other built up and strong in the Lord. I remember a couple of times of getting into my car and there was a smell of floral fragrance!

One of the last times we met up, just before lockdown in the UK, the weather had started to change quite dramatically. The sun had come out after a very long dark, wet winter. Pink and white blossom had started to cover the trees. There was a real sense that the seasons were changing. I remember mentioning to Fi, the verse from Song of Solomon chapter 2 verse 11:-

"See! The winter has passed; the rains are over and gone. Flowers appear on the earth, the season of singing has come!"

I knew in my spirit the climate both physically and spiritually had changed. I said to Fi that the blossom on the trees is a sign of the fruit that is coming later in the year at harvest time. That week, Fi had just had her beautiful engagement ring returned from having been sent off for repair as it had been damaged as a result of the seizures she had suffered. This had arrived back earlier than expected and so was back on her finger, sparkling, next to her wedding ring, just in time for her 42nd birthday. Interestingly, an engagement ring is the promise of what is yet to come! As we wait now in this new season, all that has been sown months ago will start to bear fruit.

It has been an honour to stand with Fi during this season; she has shown me what steadfast faith looks like in the face of dark news. Whilst many people are in fear at this time, while coronavirus sweeps the world, it is time to stand like she is doing and place our trust and faith in what God says.

I know one day God will fulfill the vision of going in to the prison and releasing the love of the Father over the prisoners and that a great revival is coming!

All God had in store will come to pass and just like Fi is doing, it will happen when we fix our eyes on Him!

The best is yet to come and we wait in eager anticipation!"

He's Ordering My Steps

Throughout this journey, I have seen the hand of God on every detail. I have sent regular prayer requests and praise reports to those who have committed to stand with me on the field and we have been able to rejoice together in all the victories along the way.

It was recommended that following surgery, alongside still taking anti-seizure medication and hormone tablets, an intense course of radio and chemotherapy would be embarked upon. This would involve attending the hospital Monday to Friday every day for six weeks.

Wednesday 8th January, I sent a request for prayer covering and I heard back from a good friend and faithful brother in the Lord, Gandhi, aka, *'Gands'*. His response to my message read:-

> *"You are coming to our department tomorrow. I will meet you. God is with us. We will pray."*

I had a rough recollection that Gands worked in the hospital but it turned out that this brother is a senior radiographer. Only God! I first met him in 2015 when I was out with another brother, doing some street evangelism in Southampton and Gands was also reaching out telling people about Jesus. We subsequently spent some time fellowshipping together.

If I had not been out that Saturday back in 2015, I would not have met Gands and in turn would not have had the wonderful link, my steps ordered by the Lord, for this more recent season. The last time I saw Gands would have been 2017.

Returning to Thursday 9th January 2020, we had to attend the radiotherapy department for a treatment planning session. Upon entry to the department, heaviness attempted to present itself and I recall seeing people laid out with their heads on partners shoulders, many bald, beaten up and scarred by what can only be described as a result of a foul weapon from the pit of hell. The Holy Spirit reassured me once again that we were simply walking *through* this process and directed me not to sit in any of the waiting areas as I did not belong there.

One of my *'dancing sisters',* Grace, shared with me that she felt strongly in her spirit that I was to simply turn up daily in the department and the glory of God would be revealed.

I can testify that through the whole six weeks of attending the department daily for treatment, I did not once sit down or even lean against a wall. At no point had I felt weak or even remotely tired, despite also being treated with chemotherapy and other medications.

Mix up of Names

"Fiona Wilkinson, would you like to come through please?"

I have never liked the name "Fiona" and have not used it since Pete and I got married in 2001. I have often said to Pete that if it was not for my dad having gone home to glory, I would have talked to him and my mum about changing it by deed poll but this does not sit right now. So for this short season, and *only* when dealing with the hospital, the old name had to be used as this was what matched my NHS records (gritted teeth all the way).

Whilst waiting to be called through I stood over by the doors. In came an elderly man with a lanyard and called the name *"Wilkinson"*, to which I raised my hand. He explained he was going to the toilet and would be back for me. I had assumed he was a porter and would be take me through to where I needed to go. Upon his swift return he came and greeted me, again confirming the name of '*Wilkinson*' to which I made eye contact and was ready to follow. This time, I was joined by an elderly man who was relieved his transport had arrived. This is so typical of something I would do and then find funny.

A trip to the mould room was the first port of call whereupon I was greeted by two members of staff. A mask was made to fit my head to make sure that I did not move and remained in the same position during the treatment that was to follow.

Gands accompanied us down a corridor of the department en route to our next *'sit down'*, whereupon I nullified every side effect that would seek to come near me in the Mighty Name of Jesus. Gands and myself came into agreement and declared these null and void in Jesus Name!

We then had to sit and once again be talked through the *'apparent side effects'* that I would experience as a result of chemotherapy. It was becoming quite tiresome to constantly be listening to the threats of the enemy when it should by now have been obvious that I was not accepting any of it! This radiographer was no doubt a little bemused that I had no questions and did not wish to engage in any conversation with him. During the time we were with him, he attempted to pass me literature about Macmillan, of course just part of his normal routine, but I simply replied *"No thank you!"* *(I would not be needing them).* Before heading home, I was taken through for another CT scan ahead of treatment commencing two weeks later.

Upon arriving home, I received a message from Gands to say:-

"Nice to see you today. God will do miracles in your life and will heal you completely, making you a testimony among everyone. Amen"

My mum said that whilst we were at the department, she also had a very strong sense whilst praying for me, of *"You do not belong there."*

A Cry for Revival and the Upper Room

Sunday 12th January was awesome; no two meetings at Victory Gospel church are ever the same. The only given is the 10am kick off. The Holy Spirit is always given the freedom to move and this week was no different. Having preached about being positioned for purpose, Pastor Andrew had invited everyone to come forward if they wanted to pray for revival for our land.

The majority of the church went forward and what happened next was incredible. I remember standing with my arms in the air and feeling the fire of God touch my whole being. I remember crying out to God in a new authoritative tongue and I knew in my spirit that this was for revival to hit the prisons, especially HMP Winchester.

This crying out to God went on for some time and then Pastor Josh laid his hands upon my head and prayed for the fire of God to touch my life. Again, I remember praying out in a new tongue. What I love is that the Holy Spirit touched me, prior to Pastor Josh even laying his hand on my head. Looking back, I find it funny that I had not been nervous of someone laying their hands on my head despite having only recently had staples removed after surgery.

When I returned to my seat another brother came over and said he had a Word from the Lord. He took my hands and told me that I would be laying *my* hands on the sick and they would recover overnight. He said he had been standing near me at the front when we were crying out for revival and the Holy Spirit had spoken to Him.

Throughout the winter months, our church had become part of a network of local churches to open their doors to rough sleepers to stay the night and be fed. Tuesday 21st January was one of these nights. Pete was busy with youth runs for Beth and Anna and so my brother Lloyd came to pick me up. Since the downstairs area of the church building was being used to house and care for the homeless, the prayer meeting shifted to upstairs in what I can only describe as the '*Upper Room*' prayer meeting. There were approximately twenty-five people there and I have never been to a prayer meeting like this one:-

When the Day of Pentecost had fully come,
they were all with one accord in one place.
And suddenly there came a sound from
heaven, as of a rushing mighty wind, and it
filled the whole house where they were sitting.
Then there appeared to them divided tongues,
as of fire, and one sat upon each of them.
And they were all filled with the Holy Spirit
and began to speak with other tongues, as the
Spirit gave them utterance.
(Acts 2 v 1-4)

Tuesday nights with Faith and Elaine were the closest experience to this night. The power of God fell in a tangible way and lives were transformed. It was a very precious time and I believe very significant for the days to come for the church as a whole, especially with regard to us serving the broken, ex offenders, many of these homeless and in need of unconditional love.

A Living Testimony

For the Lord Almighty has purposed, and who can thwart him?   His hand is stretched out, and who can turn it back?
(Isaiah 14 v 27)

On Saturday 18th January a letter arrived from the hospital. Seeing this was not an '*appointment*' letter, I handed it to Pete as I had no reason or desire to fill my head with lies. Pete informed me that this letter had summarised what the medics had already spoken out over my life and this basically said that my healing would not be coming from the hospital.

The Monday after the letter of apparent *'demise'* had presented itself *pleading* for my attention and acceptance, Catherine and I had the folder with every piece of paper and information booklet connected to this evil assignment out on the floor. Please note I have never read any of this! We placed the Word of God literally on top of it and cancelled every written word that had been *spoken* out over me when dictated and then sent to my address. In the Spirit, we returned the letter to sender – boldly declaring 'Not known at this address'.   We simply then declared what the Word of God had to say about the matter as Jesus did when confronted by the devil; ***"It is written!"*** There were two narratives attempting to run alongside each other and over my life. One was a lie and the other the Truth.

Again, unmoved by this devilish attempt to rob my family, I continued with my day, despite the rest of the household feeling somewhat heavy. Filthy liar! Right through this valley, whenever the enemy has sought to do his worst, at least two or three tangible blessings would always follow in hard after; oh the grace of God!

I have already shared about when Pastor Dennis was told to wait in his car ahead of receiving the news of my dad unexpectedly being called home back in 2013. On the afternoon of this Saturday, Pastor Dennis called me to say that he had been in Norway and was due to board a plane to return to the UK. Something told him not to board the plane and to remain where he was. Not knowing why this was, but knowing it was the Lord, he was obedient to the prompting of the Holy Spirit and returned to his hotel room. After taking a rest, he went for a walk during which he was expressing his immense gratitude to God for being able to walk. (*A year back, he had died and miraculously been brought back to life; this is his testimony to share. I look forward to the day myself and Pastor Dennis stand on the same platform together*).

He reported that as he was walking, I came straight into his spirit and he felt he was called as a '*General*' in the faith, to walk *through* the valley of the shadow of death with me. We had a wonderful time of fellowship and rejoicing over the goodness of God and then spent time walking through **Hebrews 11** together. Pastor Dennis explained that through our conversation, he could hear my faith had developed to a place of prophetic faith. In the Bible, prophecy is a manifestation of a form of special revelation. It means that you speak words or ideas that God has given specifically to you.

Pastor Dennis said for me to start prophesying over my ministry. I started doing this and by mid-February 2019, the Holy Spirit very clearly directed me to start writing this book. Having just scraped through my education, and definitely being the least well educated within the family, this seemed a daunting task. However, I knew that in keeping with all that had preceded I simply needed to keep walking this out in obedience and He would provide all that was necessary.

Pastor Dennis later sent me a song, '*Jesus paid it all*'; some of the lyrics are set out below:-

> *I hear the saviour say*
> *Thy strength indeed is small*
> *Child of weakness watch and pray*
> *Find in me thine all in all;*
> *Jesus paid it all; All to him I owe*
> *Sin had left a crimson stain*
> *He washed it white as snow*
>
> *Lord, now indeed I find*
> *Thy power and thine alone*
> *Came and changed the lepers spots*
> *And it melt the heart of stone*
>
> *And when before the throne*
> *I stand in him complete*
> *Jesus died my soul to save*
> *My lips shall still repeat*

> *Oh, praise the one who paid my debt*
> *And raised this life up from the dead*

Just as the Lord had literally raised Pastor Dennis from the dead, my mortal frame was being resurrected. Hallelujah! Christ had won the victory for me and because death could not hold Him down, the same applied for me. I died with Him on the cross and the very same power that raised Jesus from the dead, was resurrecting me. Victory would be all I would be speaking as this was the Truth.

> *And if the Spirit of him who raised Jesus*
> *from the dead is living in you, he who raised*
> *Christ from the dead will also give life to your*
> *mortal bodies because of his Spirit*
> *who lives in you.*
> *(Romans 8 v 11)*

Jesus had set me free and every chain had been broken off me. The Lion of Judah had roared over my life and declared the grave had no claim on me. There had been a confrontation but death had *lost* its grip.

> *So if the Son sets you free,*
> *you will be free indeed.*
> *(John 8 v 36)*

Don't Ask Why, Ask What

At no point have I asked why the events commencing on Thursday 28th November 2019 had to happen. The manifestations of the glory of God throughout this process have been obvious. As I have yielded to His will and purpose for this season, God has been touching so many lives and His glory has been, is being and will continue to be revealed. I have been strengthened so that I could endure and I can then help others.

On Saturday 25th January, I had a visit from my dear sister, Rita. She had done a two day dry fast for me, meaning she had abstained from all food and water to seek the Lord for my complete healing and deliverance. Her brother, Raphael, and cousin, Vera, from Switzerland had also joined her on this two day dry fast. I was so touched that not only Rita was doing this, which is no small thing, (from my experience fasting food for half a day is hard enough!), but she had two fellow warriors alongside her. One of them had commented that my faithfulness and unshakeable faith has been rewarded by God and that I was being taken to a new level.

Upon her arrival, after approximately an hour's drive, Rita testified to not even feeling remotely tired, having no hint of a headache and having worked through the previous day. She said the energy the Lord had given her when she was fasting and praying for me was *"extraordinary"*.

During her fast, the prayer in her heart had been *'Jesus, thou son of David, have mercy on Fi'*.

> **He called out, "Jesus, Son of David, have mercy on me!"**
>
> **Those who led the way rebuked him and told him to be quiet, but he shouted all the more, "Son of David, have mercy on me!"**
>
> **Jesus stopped and ordered the man to be brought to him. When he came near, Jesus asked him, "What do you want me to do for you?"**
>
> **"Lord, I want to see," he replied.**
>
> **Jesus said to him, "Receive your sight; your faith has healed you." Immediately he received his sight and followed Jesus, praising God. When all the people saw it, they also praised God.**
>
> **(Luke 18 v 38-43)**

Rita said she felt so energised and thankful to Jesus, our Prince of Peace. She shared that the previous night, she had a dream in which we started singing the following song:-

> **I the Lord of sea and sky**
> **I have heard my people cry**
> **All who dwell in dark and sin**
> **My hand will save**
> **I have made the stars of night**
> **I will make their darkness bright**

Who will bear my light to them?
Whom shall I send?

Here I am Lord
Is it I Lord?
I have heard You calling in the night
I will go Lord
If You lead me

I will hold Your people in my heart

I the Lord of wind and flame
I will tend the poor and lame
I will set a feast for them
My hand will save
Finest bread I will provide
Till their hearts be satisfied
I will give my life to them
Whom shall I send?

Rita and I spent a wonderful time rejoicing about the destiny and call upon my life. I am completely persuaded that part of what is ahead for me involves greater interaction with '*His boys*'. There is a call on my life to minister to these individuals in a greater capacity. Many of these are sat, hopeless, waiting in darkness. I know it is not the plan of the Father to leave them sitting in this condition. Jesus endured the cross and all that went with that in order to redeem these individuals. Despite knowing all the suffering He would have to endure, He still went to the cross, offering full and complete salvation to all who would call on His Name.

If you declare with your mouth, "Jesus is Lord," and believe in your heart that God raised him from the dead, you will be saved. For it is with your heart that you believe and are justified, and it is with your mouth that you profess your faith and are saved. As Scripture says, "Anyone who believes in him will never be put to shame." For there is no difference between Jew and Gentile—the same Lord is Lord of all and richly blesses all who call on him, for, "Everyone who calls on the name of the Lord will be saved. How, then, can they call on the one they have not believed in? And how can they believe in the one of whom they have not heard? And how can they hear without someone preaching to them? And how can anyone preach unless they are sent? As it is written: "How beautiful are the feet of those who bring good news!"

(Romans 10 v 9-15)

Before Rita left, she broke her two day fast with me (*as did Raphael and Vera*) and we shared communion together, spending a powerful time praying together in the Spirit.

Through this experience the Lord has allowed me to walk through, I have always known there is no possibility of returning to anything vaguely resembling '*lukewarm*' Christianity. How dry, boring and lifeless... There is so much more to life in Christ. The fire in my heart has been re-ignited and by the grace of God, will only continue to become brighter and hotter resulting in the extension of the Kingdom of God. The old school gospel; not watered down or sugar coated; no gimmicks or caffeine required; no requirements to keep a crowd entertained and check they stay listening; just simply the presence of the precious Holy Spirit given the time and space to move. This gospel will never wear old or become ineffective, the blood of Jesus always being sufficient for the cleansing and forgiveness of all sin and the healing of all sickness.

Work Out Your Own Salvation

Stagnant, declining or growing – what condition is your faith in? We are all individually accountable to God as to how we walk out our relationship with Him. What is to follow may not make sense to a lot of people reading and could potentially lead to offence. (Clearly this is not my intention at all – I am simply writing *my* story.)

The Lord told me at the beginning of this journey not to allow *everyone* near me for this season. He spoke to me about when He raised the little girl from the dead and had to get certain people out of the room.

> *When Jesus entered the synagogue leader's house and saw the noisy crowd and people playing pipes, he said, "Go away. The girl is not dead but asleep." But they laughed at him. After the crowd had been put outside, he went in and took the girl by the hand, and she got up. News of this spread through all that region."*
> *(Matthew 9 v 25 – 26)*

I was not to associate or even fellowship with certain people for this season; these would include, the *'mourners'*, the *'doubters'*, the *'well-wishers'*, the *'we can only hope for the best'* people and the *'all we can do is pray'* people. I did not need to "*Amen*" their *'hope-so prayers'*. There was potential for misunderstanding but this was a path I had been told to walk and I was determined to stay tuned in to the leading of the Holy Spirit whilst on the tightrope. I was to trust Him to lead me through and He would take care of the rest.

As will now be clear, I had an absolute assurance from the very beginning of this journey that I was coming through, but not everybody understood this.

Some of these people were the very ones God had warned me of at the start, to not mix with them for this season and to not reason or explain my position. This would and did require endless grace.

I remember one person not realising quite how intense the treatment was and upon me answering their question, their reaction was somewhat disappointing to me; it is sad that religion tries to make provision '*in case it doesn't work*'. However, the Holy Spirit was leaving no base uncovered. I had to forgive this person for their seemingly faithless response and leave God to deal with this. My attitude had to stay right before God. I did not have to fellowship with everyone during this season and in fact the Holy Spirit had told me not to. You cannot take people where you have not been; do not let where someone else is determine where you are.

There have also been occasions where it felt like I was challenged as to whether I have heard from God: how could I be so sure? I have also been challenged around the area of whether those supporting me on the battlefield have also heard. I have had to learn to stay quiet at times and leave God to sort these details.

The Holy Spirit also instructed me to hold back from a particular friend just for a season, a specialist nurse *'in the field'*. After she had heard about things, I received an email where she stated her concern for me. I understood the heart behind her message but knowing what she was speaking out over me was not in any way helpful or accurate. She went on to explain *her concerns*; she feared I was doing too much and explained that she wanted me to desperately be back to my normal, energetic, inspirational self but was worrying that I would be suffering from post-operative fatigue and side effects from treatment. Anyone that has seen me during this season will vouch for the fact that I have had no side effects; not even a hint of tiredness, let alone fatigue. This is my God and it is all completely miraculous. The *'normal, energetic, inspirational self'*, has never left the building! Contact with this lady was temporarily put on hold but as a good friend, and partner in the gospel, even as I write, this relationship has now resumed as it was always going to in due season. Some may find this hard to understand as after all, surely this was a God-given opportunity for me to have a *'specialist'* friend freely available for me to question whenever I liked? Whilst I understand that other people may have appreciated this, I was not walking that walk.

From the beginning, the Holy Spirit spoke clearly to me about the language I used. I was not to *'take ownership'* of anything the devil tried to pass my way. The *'parcel'* the enemy had sent my way, was not to be referred to as *'mine'* and I had at no point *'signed' to confirm receipt.* The medication was not to be called '*mine*'. The word '*my*' was replaced with '*the*'.

The Battlefield

"My feet on the battleground, my weapon will be my sound, I will not be silent, my song is my triumph."

My sister Faith likened this battle to a stage production. Stage left; and on comes the enemy with his wares; with only one intention; every foul weapon forged to kill, steal and destroy; death. Enter stage right; on comes the fullness of the Godhead, Father, Son and Holy Spirit; and abundant life. Hallelujah!

So I had to stand face to face with '*Goliath*' and had to walk through the valley of the *shadow* of death whilst knowing that the Lord had taken hold of me and put me with Him out of harm's way. I had no fear and knew I was coming through in complete victory. I was climbing to higher ground with my shield and my sword and this was not territory the enemy had *any* right to be on.

Sovereign Lord, my strong deliverer,
you shield my head in the day of battle.
(Psalm 140 v 7)

On three different occasions, I have been told by various people through this trial, that they have seen me with a huge sword and shield; 'warrior' Fi, with my feet on the neck of the enemy.

Who is on the Lord's side?
Who will serve the King?
Who will be His helpers, other lives to bring?
Who will leave the world's side?

Who will face the foe?
Who is on the Lord's side? Who for Him will go?
By Thy call of mercy, by Thy grace divine,
We are on the Lord's side—Saviour, we are Thine!

Not for weight of glory, nor for crown and palm,
Enter we the army, raise the warrior psalm;
But for love that claimeth lives for whom He died:
He whom Jesus saveth marches on His side.
By Thy love constraining, by Thy grace divine,
We are on the Lord's side—Saviour, we are Thine!

Jesus, Thou hast bought us, not with gold or gem,
But with Thine own lifeblood, for Thy diadem;
With Thy blessing filling each who comes to Thee,
Thou hast made us willing,
Thou hast made us free.
By Thy grand redemption, by Thy grace divine,
We are on the Lord's side—Saviour, we are Thine!

Fierce may be the conflict, strong may be the foe,
But the King's own army none can overthrow;
'Round His standard ranging, vict'ry is secure,
For His truth unchanging makes the triumph sure.
Joyfully enlisting, by Thy grace divine,
We are on the Lord's side—Saviour, we are Thine!

Chosen to be soldiers, in an alien land,
Chosen, called, and faithful,
for our Captain's band;
In the service royal, let us not grow cold,
Let us be right loyal, noble, true and bold.
Master, wilt Thou keep us, by Thy grace divine,
Always on the Lord's side—Saviour, always Thine!

I have never in my life experienced the feeling of being completely covered and shielded the way I did, not only by the Holy Spirit himself but also knowing *and* feeling completely surrounded by an army of faith-filled, fully trained, well-equipped soldiers, warriors and intercessors, *all* the time.

This journey has also been used for the equipping of many others. I have heard from people who have said how much my steadfast, immovable faith has inspired and encouraged them and some people are learning to wage war in the spirit realm, where previously they had not known that realm to exist, or else had no reason to battle this way before. Some of these people have come into new heights and have been encouraged and motivated to press on further into the things of God.

Through the different seasons in the valley, there were different stances and strategies used with various soldiers in position for periods of time. Once their main duties had been exercised they were able to step back and provide more of a support role.

Steven mentioned earlier how something had shifted in the prayer meeting at our house. This took a toll on both him and also on Faith. I remember Faith explaining to me one day that she needed to take a step back to regain her strength and Steven recounted feeling the same. Faith said, as in any battle, you cannot stay standing and fighting at full strength constantly; time out is required to rest, eat and regain strength ready to take another turn.

Some people that have stood with me have often felt the fiery darts themselves but have not allowed this to deter them from pressing on. By sticking with it, they have been thoroughly blessed themselves and in one case completely healed.

Joy, peace and praise were constant companions on the field. On Monday 9th December, my friend and line manager, Bethan came to visit.

Bethan writes:-

"When I visited Fi at her home, a couple of weeks after she had suffered seizures and having a diagnosis of a brain tumour, I was not sure of how she would be; I was apprehensive of saying the wrong thing or not knowing what to say at all. But the moment she opened the door, I could just see joy in her eyes. We spent time chatting and reflecting on the goodness of God. The joy Fi was carrying was God; it was so infectious. I knew at that moment that Fi would use this as a testament to point people towards Him; to show people of all backgrounds that faith can override fear in all situations. There was only a sense of faith in the conversation and no room for fear."

My brother Lloyd has told me that the supernatural joy I have experienced throughout this trial is infectious. Lloyd is an example of someone that was put into service in a very intense way, his role being for a specific season and purpose.

Lloyd writes:-

"I met Fi at Victory Gospel Church and had seen her there many times before we spoke. Despite not having engaged with her, I had always seen the joy inside her and she was always smiling; you could just see there was something different about this lady. On New Year's Eve 2019 at our celebration meeting at church, I could see the joy, happiness and peace in and on her. I could not put this into words.

Funnily enough, one day shortly after this, I received a message out the blue to say "The Hand of God is on you my brother!" When I looked at the message I could see it was from Fi. From that point onwards, we started to find out a bit more about each other's lives and I started to find out about the illness in Fi's life which to my amazement, I could not even tell that she was going through this trauma and would still not know to this day unless she had told me.

The more we have spoken, the more the joy would flow into me and I have spent a lot of time laughing to myself over the phone and at work, sometimes on occasions that Fi did not even know about, by just remembering some of the messages and voice notes. I have prayed for her day and night; sometimes I would voice note; other times I would not but I would always pray for her. Knowing what has been going on in Fi's life, many people would have crumbled; would have been depressed; would have been sad; would have experienced a time of misery and would not have smiled or even said "hello" to people. I have never seen or heard this change in her once; I have never seen sadness in her life from the minute I first saw her and then met her; all I have witnessed is joy. I knew there was something different about Fi and the joy that was in her life. I feel moved by the Presence of the Lord in her, all the time.

During this time of coronavirus, the whole world is at a standstill but Fi is still not moved; she is still smiling, singing, praising and worshipping the Lord. It is wonderful to see that she just rejoices in the midst of a storm.

I have done various things in my life; I have spent 8 years in the Royal Marines; worked as a doorman, met some amazing people, some very, very inspirational people, some top body builders and athletes, but Fi genuinely inspires me every step of my life. I am so thankful for Fi being here for me in my time of need and I am proud of the amazing work she does.

I remember this one time, she changed my whole weekend and made me so happy; she got me out of a situation that would have ended badly; praise the Lord! What a bundle of joy! She could just sense in the spirit, that something was wrong and she pulled me out of a situation which nobody else could have done. Fi inspires me greatly and it is an honour to call her my friend and my sister."

Having served as a Royal Marines commando in both Afghanistan and Iraq, Lloyd always used to remind

151

me that we stay standing '*shoulder to shoulder*'. During the six week period I was attending the hospital daily, he would pray me through every treatment, sometimes whilst working up the scaffold, and then would check in after each treatment to see how it had gone. He would also send a voice clip every night praying specifically for my sleep.

On Tuesday 14th January I had another visit from Pastor Ron, this time, with his lovely wife, Pastor Margaret. We shared a beautiful time of fellowship together and talked about the marvellous peace and joy I had right from the beginning. Pastor Ron felt in his spirit that I now just had to enter into the rest that was mine, being assured that everything had been done. We talked about the full salvation we enjoyed and about the fact that this was '*perfectly perfect and completely complete*'.

> ***Christ redeemed us from the curse of the law by becoming a curse for us, for it is written: "Cursed is everyone who is hung on a pole." He redeemed us in order that the blessing given to Abraham might come to the Gentiles through Christ Jesus, so that by faith we might receive the promise of the Spirit.***
> ***(Galatians 3 v 13-14)***

This scripture tells me that I am redeemed from the curse of the law because of Jesus becoming a curse for me. The enemy however, would seek to try to put the curse of the broken law back on me, in this case in the form of sickness, resulting in premature death. He would also seek to keep me from pressing in and taking hold of all that Christ has died to make mine; legally mine!

Christ has redeemed me by His blood and I testify to its wonderworking power to thoroughly save, cleanse, heal and deliver. Hallelujah! I am saved and kept by His blood. Satan is rendered completely powerless when confronted with the blood of Jesus.

Pastors Ron and Margaret also talked about a very special daily grace, moment by moment, that they felt was on me and interestingly, Steven had just sent me a copy of portion of a letter. My dad had written this to his parents' way back many years ago:-

"God revealed Himself to Moses by the name "I Am", not "I Was" or "I Will Be". So we regret the past and worry about the future and Jesus responds when we mention yesterday, "I am not in yesterday, I am for you Now" and when we have anxieties about tomorrow, He says "I am not in tomorrow but for you now". If we don't have Him now, we don't have Him. I am the Lord and I change not. There is no shadow made by turning with me and my son, Jesus, is the same yesterday, today and forever. Yesterday is dead, tomorrow is not even born but will you know me 'Now'?"

Shortly after this, Pastor Dennis one day wrote to me:-

"The reality is that trusting God takes a whole-hearted commitment from dawn till dusk. But we are never alone in it, "And surely I am with you always to the end of the age" (Matthew 28v20). I

153

love it! God said to Moses, "I am that I am!" God wanted to assure Moses and Israel that God would become what they would need Him to become. In using the words, "I AM THAT I AM", God used an expression to reveal to Moses a promise and pledge found in His Name. That same pledge and promise is to you and me my sister because God has not changed. I will become whatsoever I may become, in Moses' case, their deliverer; in yours and mine a year ago, my healer and resurrection!"

No Weapon

They triumphed over him
by the blood of the Lamb
and by the word of their testimony
(Revelation 12 v 11)

I have always stood on the promises of God and hold
the view that if God has spoken, that settles it. I have
no reason to question or worry. He is not a man that
He should lie. All that the enemy had meant for evil,
God was turning around for good.

You intended to harm me, but God intended it
for good to accomplish what is now being
done, the saving of many lives.
(Genesis 50 v 20)

All kinds of words had been spoken out over me but
I was only listening to and speaking out words of life.

The tongue has the power of life and death,
and those who love it will eat its fruit.
(Proverbs 18:21)

Side effects *apparently* due to be heading my way
would hit my shield of faith and be extinguished in
Jesus Name and there was no weapon formed against
me that would prosper. I do not deny that these
weapons were forged, only that God was bringing me
through and would keep His promises to me. No
snare of the enemy would succeed.

No weapon forged against you will prevail,

*and you will refute every tongue
that accuses you.
This is the heritage of the servants
of the Lord,
and this is their vindication from me.
(Isaiah 54 v 17)*

As treatment commenced at the end of January, we were *not* now walking into a '*six week period of low time*' with the expectations of things looking grey and having to adjust. No; there was nothing to adjust to. Each day, like any other day, there was more than enough grace. Apart from some pretty major hair loss, a consequence of the radiotherapy, I testify that I have not experienced any side effects and felt 100% throughout, not even experiencing a hint of tiredness. *(A couple of people have commented that the hair loss due to radiation is necessary proof for some people that I had undergone such an intense experience as I do not have a mark on me).* I had sent a prayer request out to all my soldiers and warriors and this included my brother Gands. His response was:-

"I will see you tomorrow in the treatment machine. Our great God is with us. He will make you as a witness among everyone to glorify His Name. We will keep praying until the miracle happens!"

Every morning, Pete, would bring up the drugs and at my request place them on top of a scripture I had written out and stuck on the drawers next to our bed. I would declare this word aloud every time before taking anything into my body:-

They will pick up snakes with their hands;
and when they drink deadly poison, it will not
hurt them at all; they will place their hands
on sick people, and they will get well.
(Mark 16 v 18)

I would command anything entering my system to only attack and destroy rogue cells and forbade them even to go near healthy cells. If not required, to turn immediately into food to nourish my system in Jesus Name!

Every night before I went to bed, I would take communion and anoint my head with oil and declare:- *"Healed and whole in Jesus Name – set apart for His use."*

(Pete accompanied me for the daily treatment to start with and then after a week or two, my mum stepped in allowing Pete to go to work.)

Treatment Testimonies, Triumphs & Challenges

Upon arrival in the radiotherapy department on 23rd January I was met by Gands. Wherever I went, God had placed his angels all around, attendants to serve his daughter. Ironically, hair bands were a necessary requirement for my thick blond hair in these early days, in order for the mask to fit tight as you get pinned down hard. Gands joked saying he did not get to put his daughter's hair up very much anymore so attempted bunches on me, (he did okay...). I was allowed to choose a song to be played during treatment so *'Way Maker'* filled the airwaves. I declared Jesus to be '*My* Way Maker', *My* Miracle Worker, *My* Promise Keeper, *My* Light in the Darkness. This was personal. As time went on, I arrived one day to find one of the team had '*Way Maker*' on ready for me.

I had to go between two rooms for treatment and this meant seeing different members of staff. One man who I got to know quite well commented one day:- ***"We need you in this room more often as you bring so much joy with you!"*** I told him he was going to see a miracle and that God was carrying me through it all.

Other memories worth noting:-

- I was told, ***"You are sailing through this!"*** (I was in the ark after all!).
- One of the regular members of the team I had got to know well was heading home after his shift one day and when he saw me stood in the corridor waiting to be called through, stopped to give me a hug and said "*Hello special lady!*"
- One day my mum commented that she could hear "*Raise a Hallelujah*" and "*Alpha and Omega*" playing loud and clear down the corridor; the atmosphere being set and filled with truth. One of the nurses giving treatment that day commented that he recognised the song from me having played it on a previous day.
- Twice within the treatment room, members of staff had requested I please pray with them. So, holding hands at the end of the treatment machine, I remember laughing and thanking the

Lord for the opportunity to pray together. One time, two of these staff were faith-filled believers and after me having prayed for them at their request, I went on and thanked the Lord for my healing and prayed for further miracles to break out throughout the department. We all said Amen. At the end of this time, another member of staff came in and commented that the room was so joyful!

For in Him I live and move and
have MY being.
(Acts 17 v 28)

Time to shop for Beanies

A couple of weeks into radiotherapy, it was obvious that my hair was starting to fall out. Standing in the shower surrounded by sufficient hair to block a drain is tough. However, there was a very clear line of where the hair remained and I was reminded of the Nicole Mullen song:-

Who taught the sun where to
stand in the morning?
And who told the ocean
you can only come this far?
And who showed the moon
where to hide 'til evening?
Whose words alone can catch a falling star?

This was one of the many songs I had sang back on our family holiday in August whilst overlooking the sea. God has complete charge over every strand of my hair and in fact had every one numbered.

I felt strongly not to shave the good quantity of hair I had been graciously left with as after all, this was no ordinary path I was walking. The grace of God was such that, with a beanie on, even though the top of my head had been robbed I was left with more than sufficient hair around the front of my face and around the side and back.

Where I had been concerned to take a comb or brush to my head, not wanting to invite further hair loss, I had arrived in the treatment room on Thursday 20th February with extremely matted hair. The member of staff treating me that day could not position the mask without hurting my face as the hair sat blocking the way. In fact he pretty much said that if I turned up with my hair in that '*state*' tomorrow, treatment would not be an option and this could affect the 'prognosis'. I took immediate authority over these words he had just spoken out and reminded the enemy he was a liar, directing him back to the cross to survey the place where a public spectacle was made of him.

Upon returning home, I made contact with three sisters to see if they would please come over and attempt to brush these knots out for me. All of these ladies were otherwise engaged and I think deep down, I knew the only way forward was to be cut free from these unsightly tangles. Another gift of grace; I made contact with a sister, Yvonne who owned her own salon, based at home, and she said to go over as soon as I wanted and she would sort me out.

I remember the relief when she took the scissors to what can only be described as rats' nests. She commented she could see the relief in my face as she took the scissors to them. How I had endured the discomfort of having had my hair in such an uncomfortable state was a question I struggle to answer. Even in bed, they had been so uncomfortable. I now felt amazing and completely liberated. As I sat in front of her mirror, a regular customer arrived for their appointment so another opportunity for a brief share of the goodness of God. There and then, I invited this lady to hear the story. She seemed very intrigued. God had the glory even as I sat in front of a mirror having huge sections of my hair cut off before my eyes.

Charm is deceptive, and beauty is fleeting;
but a woman who fears the Lord
is to be praised.
Honour her for all that her hands have done,
and let her works bring her praise
at the city gate.
(Proverbs 31 v 30)

Looking in the mirror, and being faced with what looked back, no longer recognising who you see above the eye brows is a challenge. I had emerged from serious brain surgery with a full head of thick blond hair, as the hair they shaved for this procedure was so minimal. As I write this section, all I see is a bald head, but surrounded by the sides and back with the original hair.

My eyes and skin, however, have glowed throughout the journey and you will read witness accounts of this.

I have had most hair styles in my time from straight long hair to perms, growing it back out then deciding one day to go for the '*Annie Lennox*' style plus getting razored at the back. I still remember my dad's face upon first seeing this. I then grew this style out in time for our wedding. I can now have the opportunity to go through all these styles again and decide what I like. I look forward to the day when my hair is long enough for Anna to once again create the look I loved, the inverted French plaits. *(This will be some time yet)*.

One day was particularly challenging as a nurse really struggled to take my blood. Having failed with one arm, she moved on to the next. Eventually, got me to bleed but having started to complete the paperwork, realised she was supposed to have taken three vials but had only taken two. Apparently once a member of staff has tried taking someone's blood twice, they have to hand this on to someone else. So at this point, a more senior member of staff is called upon. Half way through yet *another* failed attempt at getting me to bleed, we were told we were to leave the room as it was now required for recovery purposes so a patient was wheeled in and we were moved out. Upon arrival in our new location and half way through the procedure, this nurse was left with one final attempt. After him searching round for pillows and paper towels, he need not have bothered as this resulted in yet another failed attempt. Just as he said he would have to get someone else as he could not try a third time, we saw the funny side and I said enough was enough for one day; I was not having anyone else near me. I suggested it was like it was like an episode of the 1970's sitcom, '*Some Mothers Do 'Ave 'Em'*, having to keep being moved around the building. He agreed and we laughed together. Upon leaving the room, he jokingly asked me whether there was anywhere else in the department I would like to see as we seem to have started a tour. I declined his offer and headed home.

Once during treatment, I was asked by a nurse if I was on steroids as apparently I looked "*so well*". Towards the end of treatment, the nurses commented how good the skin on my head looked and asked what I was using on it. They were surprised to find it was only E45 lotion. They said the scar across my head was neat and that it was "*very unusual*" to see someone looking so well. One day, due to the heavy rain, I ran from the building following treatment all the way back to the car, having boundless energy.

On the second to last day of radiotherapy running alongside chemo and I bumped into the lady that had made the mask all those weeks back. She commented how well I looked too and, again, was surprised when I told her I had no side effects from treatment.

When I got home that morning, I was delighted to find a beautiful bouquet of flowers from my prison team sat on the doorstep waiting for me. This was to thank me for leading the team through the course. I always tell them I could not do it without them and am so grateful for them all.

On the last day of radiotherapy, a nurse commented that it was most unusual for me to look and feel so well. They told me my eyes were bright and that my face was literally glowing; they stood amazed and asked what I was taking on the side!

> *The eye is the lamp of the body. If your eyes*
> *are healthy, your whole body will be*
> *full of light.*
> *(Matthew 6 v 22)*

One of them asked if I thought my faith in Jesus helped me get through and I told her yes, without a doubt. She smiled and said it was amazing. I told them that I would be inviting the whole department to come and hear the whole story starting about when I was pulled from the car by my YP and they looked at each other and agreed they would be very interested.

Treatment Reviews

I had to attend for weekly treatment reviews and also for bloods to be taken. I would always wait outside the building in the fresh air until Pete called me in. At the first review, the specialist pharmacist we met with greeted me with the words:-

> *"You look full of the joys of life!"*

Second treatment review and I was greeted with the words:-

> *"You are looking so well!"*

At the review meeting on 14th February, the lady commented:-

> *"You are still looking so well!"*

As she said this, I literally felt the glory of God from the top of my forehead down to my chin.

At another review on Friday 28th February I was told the skin on my head looked really good and the pharmacist was again clearly surprised that I *still* had no side effects. Conversations would go something like:-

"Any nausea?"

"I have had no side effects!"

"Any vomiting?"

"I have had no side effects!"

(I was then told that after treatment stopping, it could take up to two weeks to not experience any side effects...)

Bloods were always reported to be excellent throughout reviews.

Fourth Man in the Fire

You, Lord, keep my lamp burning;
my God turns my darkness into light.
(Psalm 18 v 28)

Every time I entered the hospital or prison, it would feel that '*the light had been turned on*' in both places during this season.

Catherine writes (again):-

"Your boldness and faith is so inspiring and is affecting the hospital atmosphere! Your light in there is dispelling the darkness. Your testimony is a witness to the unbelievers and this is having an amazing effect. The devil will soon be sorry he touched you because you have gone to another level of impact. He thought he could bring you down with fear and sickness but instead you have risen up with power from on high and declared war on his territory! Thank you Jesus for all you are doing with Fi; she is your walking testimony and light."

But thanks be to God, who always leads us as captives in Christ's triumphal procession and uses us to spread the aroma of the knowledge of him everywhere. For we are to God the pleasing aroma of Christ among those who are being saved and those who are perishing.
(2 Corinthians 2 v 14-15)

Now I want you to know, brothers and sisters,
that what has happened to me has actually
served to advance the gospel. As a result, it
has become clear throughout the whole
palace guard and to everyone else that I am in
chains for Christ. And because of my chains,
most of the brothers and sisters have become
confident in the Lord and dare all the more to
proclaim the gospel without fear.
(Phillipians 1 v 12- 14)

In early February, Pastor Josh had prayed for me and thanked the Lord for me having gone into the hospital and been the light. He gave thanks that I had been able to minister and reach out to the people that were meant to be looking after me and for the fact that God had surrounded me with saints and believers.

He thanked the Lord for the light that was inside of me and prayed that this light would just keep getting stronger and stronger in Jesus' Name. He reminded the devil that his plan to take me out and bring me into a place of darkness had failed and that all that had happened was that I brought light to a place of darkness. He went on to rebuke the devil and decreed and declared that life would be my portion and that everywhere where I go, I would be a spreader of light, touching many hearts and lives and to many people sat in dark situations, I would give testimony to say:-

"Look what the Lord has done for me; he has
saved and redeemed my life, he kept me!"

167

He prophesied that I be like a city on a hill that all may see and that all may know, looking upon my life and saying:-

"Surely there is a God in heaven who loves, who cares, who heals, who saves, who redeems, who delivers!"

For he is the living God and he endures forever; his kingdom will not be destroyed, his dominion will never end. He rescues and he saves; he performs signs and wonders in the heavens and on the earth. He has rescued Daniel from the power of the lions."

So Daniel prospered during the reign of Darius and the reign of Cyrus the Persian.

(Daniel 6)

Daniel was preserved by faith and is mentioned in the book of Hebrews as one who, by faith, stopped the mouths of lions. Daniel had been plotted against, but still he prayed and praised; this was just who he was and what he did. He was preserved, and then he prospered and was shown favour.

Then the herald loudly proclaimed, "Nations and peoples of every language, this is what you are commanded to do: As soon as you hear the sound of the horn, flute, zither, lyre, harp, pipe and all kinds of music, you must fall down and worship the image of gold that

King Nebuchadnezzar has set up. Whoever does not fall down and worship will immediately be thrown into a blazing furnace." ... At this time some astrologers came forward and denounced the Jews. They said to King Nebuchadnezzar, "May the king live forever! Your Majesty has issued a decree that everyone who hears the sound of [the instruments] must fall down and worship the image of gold, and that whoever does not fall down and worship will be thrown into a blazing furnace. But there are some Jews whom you have set over the affairs of the province of Babylon—Shadrach, Meshach and Abednego—who pay no attention to you, Your Majesty. They neither serve your gods nor worship the image of gold you have set up."...Furious with rage, Nebuchadnezzar summoned Shadrach, Meshach and Abednego. So these men were brought before the king, and Nebuchadnezzar said to them, "Is it true, Shadrach, Meshach and Abednego, that you do not serve my gods or worship the image of gold I have set up? Now when you hear the sound of the [instruments] if you are ready to fall down and worship the image I made, very good. But if you do not worship it, you will be thrown immediately into a blazing furnace. Then what god will be able to rescue you from my hand?" [They] replied to him, "King Nebuchadnezzar, we do not need to defend ourselves before you in this matter. If we are thrown into the blazing furnace, the God we serve is able to deliver us from it, and he will deliver us from Your Majesty's hand... Then Nebuchadnezzar was furious with [them] and his attitude toward them changed. He ordered the furnace heated seven times hotter than usual and commanded some of the strongest soldiers in his army to tie [them up] and throw them into the blazing furnace. So these men, wearing their robes, trousers, turbans and other clothes, were bound and thrown into the blazing furnace. The king's command was so urgent and the furnace so hot that the flames of the fire killed the soldiers who took [them up] and these three men, firmly tied, fell into the blazing furnace. Then King Nebuchadnezzar leaped to his feet in amazement and asked his advisers, "Weren't there three men that we tied up and threw into the fire? They replied, "Certainly, Your Majesty." He said, "Look! I see four men walking around in the fire, unbound and unharmed, and the fourth looks like a son of the gods."

Nebuchadnezzar then approached the opening of the blazing furnace and shouted, "Shadrach, Meshach and Abednego, servants of the Most High God, come out! Come here! So [they] came out of the fire... They saw that the fire had not harmed their bodies, nor was a hair of their heads singed; their robes were not scorched, and there was no smell of fire on them. Then Nebuchadnezzar said, "Praise be to the God of Shadrach, Meshach and Abednego, who has sent his angel and rescued his servants! They trusted in him and defied the king's command and were willing to give up their lives rather than serve or worship any god except their own God... Then the king promoted Shadrach, Meshach and Abednego in the province of Babylon.

(Daniel 3)

The three Hebrew boys went into the fire and come out unscathed. They knew their God and did not need proof before they accepted that something was true and consequently received the favour of the King.

I have been in and through the fire and testify to the presence of the fourth man being with me continually.

Business as Usual

The first Sycamore Tree course of 2020 kicked off properly at the end of January. Just before heading off that lunchtime, Pastor Andrew called and prayed for me. He said that when I went in to the prison full of the presence of God, the men would see His glory radiating from me as I would be filled to overflowing.

He said to me, "You are my servant,
Israel, in whom I will display my splendour."
(Isaiah 49 v 3)

My mum kindly drove me to and from the prison every week. I would meet Mike, my official '*bag carrier*' for this course nearby and then we would walk and meet the rest of the team; a fully supportive and thoroughly equipped group of fellow volunteers; Rachel, Lynne, Jacqui, Jane, John, Rod and Peter. What a dream team this turned out to be.

Before the twenty new course recruits arrived in the chapel I was moved to see our two peer mentors appear. The chaplaincy team had taken the decision to tell these two men a little about what had been going on for me since the last course. These two men were so lovely in expressing their genuine care and concern for me. The last time I had seen them was the day before the 'confrontation'. One of the men said he had been praying for me since he had heard. They had also written me a card, thanking me for all the support I had given them both and saying they were looking forward to working with me on future courses. This is pegged on my office board alongside another card from all the boys from a previous course, thanking me and my wonderful team for the impact we have had on them. These cards are so special and I will always treasure them.

During that afternoon, one of the new recruits said goodbye at the end of the session and said he would definitely be returning next week to see "*that smile!*" Being a *'young looking middle aged female'* within an all-male environment does tend to attract the occasional comment and attention, however, after some banter and mutual respect we have a great working relationship. This boy had seen something on me.

> ***Then all the peoples on earth will see that you are called by the name of the Lord, and they will fear you.***
> ***(Deuteronomy 28 v 10)***

On the last Wednesday in February the treatment machine was due to receive a service so a well-earned day off for me. This was such a blessing since it was both Pete's birthday and also graduation day for my Sycamore Tree attendees. I had to get up extra early to take the meds and then stopped at McDonalds to grab breakfast on the way.

I remember being so grateful for the graciousness of the officer conducting the sniffer dog search upon arrival, during which I obviously had to remove my hat. I remember we shared an all too familiar but helpful joke about me still having more hair than him.

The boys on the course were lovely too. One commented that I was a soldier; I received so much respect and was even told by one inmate, that he was praying for me.

Having stood all day from 8:45am in one of my favourite places with some of my favourite people, I sat down at 5pm, not even tired. We then went on to celebrate Pete's birthday. What an awesome day this had been.

Catherine had come into the prison that day, as our team are permitted to invite members of the community in and she commented:-

"Well done Fi! You did so well and I can see you are in your element there. The graduation was very moving and I felt that significant changes have been made in those men's hearts; a truly worthwhile investment going on in there."

It's a New Season

On 1st March 2020, I had arranged to take Shane Taylor into HMP Winchester for him to share his story during the chapel service. Shane and his wife, Sam, arrived at our home the previous afternoon and stayed with us that Saturday night. This time was very relaxed and as well as sharing about the goodness of God, we had a laugh together. Upon arrival at the prison, I escorted Shane and his wife to the chapel and I was delighted to see that some of the boys from the Sycamore Tree course that had just finished that week had come to hear the story and I was able to get Shane to sign a copy of his book for them.

Shane then drove us back to base where we sat and shared a roast that Pete had prepared and we then relaxed ahead of attending a second speaking engagement I had lined up for him in the community later that afternoon.

On Tuesday 10th March I had a visit from my sister, Elaine. We had attempted to meet a couple of times previously but whenever we tried, Elaine had felt unwell.

However, this was a divine appointment. This sister arrived carrying a heavy anointing and when I invited her to take a seat, she replied:-"*I will when business has been done*". She then proceeded to share:-

He stilled the storm to a whisper;
the waves of the sea were hushed.

They were glad when it grew calm,
and he guided them to their desired haven.
(Psalm 107 v 29-30)

This spirit-filled woman of God then shared that *He* was going to '*disassociate*' me from '*that thing*', commenting that He was very aware that I had never associated myself with it all along. It had sought a strong association with me but had failed at every attempt. There was to be a severing; a permanent separation.

He will make an utter end of it.
Affliction will not rise up a second time.
(Nahum 1 v 9)

Also, my sister spoke of walls beginning to tumble. Hallelujah! These walls took various forms and ranged from walls of some people's expectations with regards how things should be; walls the enemy had sought to put up to seek to define '*his boundaries*' and also walls of '*what would normally be the case*'. These walls were all set to start tumbling in the spiritual realm and then manifest in the natural. We talked about Isaiah 30:-

A thousand will flee
at the threat of one;
at the threat of five
you will all flee away,
till you are left
like a flagstaff on a mountaintop,
like a banner on a hill.

Yet the Lord longs to be gracious to you;
therefore he will rise up to
show you compassion.
For the Lord is a God of justice.
Blessed are all who wait for him!

(Isaiah 30 v 17-18)

Elaine shared that I would receive beauty for ashes and that I would be recompensed for what I had gone through. I was to remain rejoicing at all times and to give up no ground.

Steven also shared a scripture with me with regard to recompense. There would be a full recompense for all the times spent visiting and staying in the hospital, taking medications, having my licence taken and everything else.

Therefore this is what the Lord says
concerning the king of Assyria:

"'He will not enter this city
or shoot an arrow here.
He will not come before it with shield
or build a siege ramp against it.
By the way that he came he will return;
he will not enter this city,
declares the Lord.
I will defend this city and save it,
for my sake and for the sake of
David my servant.'"

(2 Kings 19 v 32-34)

Testify

I have been told a couple of times throughout the journey by others that God the Father was pleased with me. However, there came a point where *I* started to hear and receive this direct from the Father myself. I had walked through the valley confident that He was bringing me through, fully trusting Him every time I put one foot in front of another on the tightrope and He was delighted. We often talk about delighting ourselves in the Lord and it is right we do so; however, what an awesome thought that the King of Kings and the Lord of Lords, my heavenly Father, my dad, was delighted with me.

He brought me out into a spacious place;
he rescued me because he delighted in me.
(Psalm 18 v 19)

Whoever dwells in the shelter of
the Most High
will rest in the shadow of the Almighty.
I will say of the Lord, "He is my refuge and
my fortress,
my God, in whom I trust."

Surely he will save you
from the fowler's snare
and from the deadly pestilence.
He will cover you with his feathers,
and under his wings you will find refuge;
his faithfulness will be your
shield and rampart.
You will not fear the terror of night,

nor the arrow that flies by day,
nor the pestilence that stalks in the darkness,
nor the plague that destroys at midday.

A thousand may fall at your side,
ten thousand at your right hand,
but it will not come near you.
You will only observe with your eyes
and see the punishment of the wicked.
If you say, "The Lord is my refuge,"
and you make the Most High your dwelling,
no harm will overtake you,
no disaster will come near your tent.

For he will command his angels
concerning you
to guard you in all your ways;
they will lift you up in their hands,
so that you will not strike your foot
against a stone.
You will tread on the lion and the cobra;
you will trample the great lion
and the serpent.

Because she loves me," says the Lord,
"I will rescue her;
I will protect her, for she
acknowledges my name.
She will call on me, and I will answer her;
I will be with her in trouble,
I will deliver her and honour her.
With long life I will satisfy her
and show her my salvation."

Psalm 91 v (14-16 in particular)

When I get back behind the wheel, the first trip I will be taking is into town – the exact route I took on 28th November 2019 – and I shall be rejoicing for a full and complete recovery. I have been *driven* this way as a passenger in *my* car and there is no trauma attached. We even got stopped by the lights in exactly the spot I was *confronted*. I praise the Lord that we do not need to go car shopping as I am more than a conqueror. Once I have my keys back, I have every intention of taking back full ownership of my car.

David had a willingness to face every giant put in front of Him for the glory and honour of God. As I have faced a giant, all will see and hear that there is a God on the throne reigning and no flesh can glory in His presence. Let him who glories, glory in the Lord. God is looking for a people who will rise up and say I have a promise from God and no giant or man or power of hell is going to stop me. I was walking through with a song of praise whilst moving from glory to glory; a prayer to simply survive falls far short of the glory of God. God cannot be who He is not. I always knew I would run up out of the valley victorious, I would not scrape through and crawl over the finish line. I would be running and triumphing over everything that was set up against me.

This is what the LORD *says to his anointed,*
to Cyrus, whose right hand I take hold of
to subdue nations before him
and to strip kings of their armour,
to open doors before him
so that gates will not be shut:

I will go before you
and will level the mountain;
I will break down gates of bronze
and cut through bars of iron.
I will give you hidden treasures,
riches stored in secret places,
so that you may know that I am the LORD,
the God of Israel, who summons you by
name.
(Isaiah 45 v 1-3)

My prayer is that God use me for His glory. I believed God and all the way through experienced the victory first-hand. I have not once stopped to take a look at my powerful enemies or cower before them.

The people that know their God shall be
strong, and do exploits.
(Daniel 11 v 32)

So, to recap, during the first round of treatment which involved me attending the hospital daily for six weeks, undergoing an intense course of both radiotherapy and chemo, apart from hair loss, I experienced no side effects. I tutored the Sycamore Tree course during this time too, including marking the course work.

Prior to lockdown, I had also completed another peer mentor programme within the prison. Whilst there, I had a catch up and pray with Rev Cliff McClelland where we shared about lots of encouraging things that were going on within the prison and within our own lives.

Reverend Cliff McClelland, Chaplain HMP Winchester writes:-

"I have thoroughly enjoyed working with Fi as she heads up the volunteer Sycamore Tree Course team that comes into HMP Winchester. Fi has a Godly focus and caring nature fuelled by a whirlwind of energy that ensures Jesus remains at the centre of all that she does. She is loved and respected by so many in here, which ensures her teaching is received well. Fi, following her call to serve here, results in Godly transformation for so many men."

Within this period, we had Shane and his wife come to stay for the weekend and I escorted him into HMP Winchester on the Sunday in order for him to share his testimony.

The GP had signed me off work through to at least the end of March. After what seemed a sensible time taken for recovery, by the time the end of February had arrived, it seemed obvious to me that I was fit to return to work upon expiry of this certificate (if not before; since I felt 100%, I could not justify being signed off sick).

After discussions had been had, arrangements were made for my return to work and I genuinely felt that part of the '*recompense*' was the joy that I felt around this return to my job which had been stolen. The fact I could not drive was not an issue for my managers – they just wanted me back working. In fact, once lockdown was in place, none of my colleagues were allowed to go anywhere either! Father God had

182

already gone ahead, making the crooked places straight.

At the end of March we had had a telephone appointment with the hospital pharmacist. The plan was to do six 'cycles' of chemo, increasing the dose over the first two cycles. In each twenty-eight day cycle, treatment would be given for the first five days and then twenty-three days off.

It goes without saying that once again all the side effects were spoken over my life and the pharmacist told me that having started treatment on a Monday, I would most likely be feeling very lethargic and not fit for a lot by the Thursday. I was also told that most people elect to stop the treatment before they get through all six cycles because they find the side effects too challenging. I took authority over these words that had been spoken over me and nullified them in the spirit realm.

During the next stage of chemo, once again, despite the dose being raised significantly, I experienced no side effects, returning to work at the beginning of April, the day this round of treatment commenced. I love how God works. I have written this book throughout this season, have walked miles every day, including ten miles on one day.

I will give thanks and never stop singing of His love for me. I shall walk among believers and non-believers alike as a living testimony. I will not be stopped or silenced. I was never going to stop and worship at a place that is short of full victory in Christ; never doing a deal with the devil. Why would

I settle for mediocrity when I have the full power of God at my disposal? I was not going to buy the lie that this is as far as you can come but you are to go no further.

Like David, I ran into the valley to face the giant and confounded the opposition. Something has been done so deep in my life that I have no choice but to sing and praise my God. Many will see and fear. This song cannot be found in the natural man or anywhere else in the world. The peace, joy and rest I have had continually had has not been given to me by anyone or anything in this world so nobody or nothing can take it from me.

Olly Sherwood aka King Jims (friend):-

"Fi is a ray of sunshine to all who know her, someone who is focused on using her life emanating God's love to those around her. I am encouraged by her endurance in hardship and her rejoicing in trials and I am glad to call her my sister in Christ."

Who Has The Final Say?

*With your help I can advance against a troop;
with my God I can scale a wall. As for God,
his way is perfect: The Lord's word is
flawless; he shields all who take refuge in
him. For who is God besides the Lord? And
who is the Rock except our God? It is God
who arms me with strength and keeps my way
secure. He makes my feet like the feet of a
deer; he causes me to stand on the heights.
He trains my hands for battle; my arms can
bend a bow of bronze. You make your saving
help my shield, and your right hand sustains
me; your help has made me great. You
provide a broad path for my feet, so that my
ankles do not give way. I pursued my
enemies and overtook them; I did not turn
back till they were destroyed. I crushed them
so that they could not rise; they fell beneath
my feet. You armed me with strength for
battle; you humbled my adversaries before
me. You made my enemies turn their backs
in flight, and I destroyed my foes. They cried
for help, but there was no one to save them- to
the Lord, but he did not answer. I beat them
as fine as windblown dust; I trampled them
like mud in the streets. You have delivered
me from the attacks of the people; you have
made me the head of nations. People I did not
know now serve me, foreigners cower before
me; as soon as they hear of me, they obey me.*

They all lose heart; they come trembling from their strongholds. The Lord lives! Praise be to my Rock! Exalted be God my Saviour! He is the God who avenges me, who subdues nations under me, who saves me from my enemies. You exalted me above my foes; from a violent man you rescued me. Therefore I will praise you, Lord, among the nations; I will sing the praises of your name. He gives his king great victories; he shows unfailing love to his anointed, to David and to his descendants forever.

(Psalm 18 v 29-50)

He had armed me with strength in my heart and hands such that not one of my enemies was able to rise up against me. He had enabled me to tread on serpents and nothing had by any means hurt me. This had never been a physical battle and was only ever going to be won by the Spirit of God working within me and this by my faith in the finished work of Christ. All that heaven possesses has been made mine. I had triumphed over every demonic force that had sought to triumph over me. He had caused me to bend a bow of bronze and has been preparing me for higher ground upon which I will be used to escort others out from the dungeons and demonic places where the enemy has people bound.

God's right hand had not only strengthened and sustained me, but had also enabled me to be shaped and fashioned for the territory I was shortly to embark upon.

It did not matter what the enemy put in front of me as I was not looking for any natural way of getting over. In my weakness, He was made strong. I overcame that what was trying to overcome me. No matter how strong the power of the weapon of the enemy *appears* to be, it is just a show, since the devil has already been defeated. None of his filthy weapons have any permanent power.

But he said to me, "My grace is sufficient for you, for my power is made perfect in weakness." Therefore I will boast all the more gladly about my weaknesses, so that Christ's power may rest on me.
(2 Corinthians 12 v 9)

Due to lockdown, when I have needed to have bloods taken, this has simply involved a walk to the GP surgery and when I first attended at the beginning of April, nurse Kerry commented how well I looked. Curious at this statement, I asked her what she meant and she said that my face, eyes and skin were glowing and I told her it was a miracle. She was also amazed at the fact I was walking for miles.

On one occasion, before leaving the room, I asked her if she would like me to pray for her to which she replied "*Yes please*" and so right after having my bloods taken, I prayed a very simple prayer with her.

During the follow up virtual appointment, the pharmacist reported that my bloods were all excellent and was again very surprised that I was *still* doing so well. Upon telling her that I had experienced no side effects despite them having doubled the dose, that I wished she could see me to see how well I looked, she commented that she did not need to as she could literally hear how well I was from down the phone! I told her that the nurse at the GP surgery had commented that I was glowing. She thought it was amazing. It was no surprise when she asked once again whether I had suffered with nausea or vomiting. I told her no, and also informed her that if anything, my energy levels had increased. This resulted in her asking what dose of steroids I was taking these days as these can obviously affect your mood. This lady knows I have not taken any steroids since December. She could not reason this and I was able to share with her that I was walking several miles a day, that I was back at work and had almost finished writing a book. She asked what the book was about and I explained that from the beginning of this, I knew that God was bringing me through and also shared a little about my heart for the broken, particularly my heart for prisoners. We talked about this for a while and I told her it was all a complete miracle. She genuinely seemed very pleased and said that I would have to invite her and all the staff I had dealt with to the '*book launch*'. It had been prophesied over me that He would be a wall of fire around me and the glory in my midst.

At the start of May, the chemo dose was increased as planned and I report no side effects. This was the maximum dose now and would not be increased. *(Every time these meds are delivered to our home, the first thing I do is completely destroy any paperwork, even if this is just a sticky label, referring to me as a*

*'cancer patient' and take authority over these words;
the devil is a liar).*

The next telephone appointment with the pharmacist
(29th May) was held on Portsmouth seafront since the
weather was outstanding and everyone was off school
and work. I was told once again that my bloods had
all come back excellent and the pharmacist was
astounded that despite now being on the maximum
dose, I was still experiencing no side effects. All the
usual questions were asked again and once again, I
was challenged as to what dose of steroids I was on!
I told her I found it funny that she asked me this every
time we had a review and every time my answer is
the same. I then went on to report that I had almost
finished my book, had walked ten miles and had done
some extra hours at work. She was bemused to say
the least. I testified to feeling one hundred percent
well and feel no different when I am on treatment to
when I am not on it. Following the appointment, I
had to walk at speed to catch up with the family.

As He is, so are we in this world.
(1 John 4 v 17)

I was invited to attend the hospital for an MRI scan
of my head on Saturday 13th June at 9:45am. All the
staff involved with the MRI scan were handpicked by
the Lord. I was seen early and scanned whilst
listening to a playlist of songs filled with truth that the
radiographer had sorted himself for me, having told
him just one song to start off with.

In the week leading up to the scan, a sister gave me
the following scripture;-

I will exalt you, my God the King;
I will praise your name forever and ever.

Every day I will praise you
and extol your name forever and ever.

Great is the Lord and most worthy of praise;
his greatness no one can fathom.
One generation commends your
works to another;
they tell of your mighty acts.
They speak of the glorious splendour
of your majesty—
and I will meditate on your wonderful works.
They tell of the power
of your awesome works—
and I will proclaim your great deeds.
They celebrate your abundant goodness
and joyfully sing of your righteousness.

(Psalm 145 v 1-7)

I read around different versions of this and was so encouraged to read The Message version of verses 6 & 7 in particular.

Your marvellous doings are headline news;
I could write a book full of the details
of your greatness.

The fame of your goodness spreads
across the country;
your righteousness is on everyone's lips.

(Psalm 145 v 6-7, The Message)

It was prophesied very early on that my head would be the talk of the hospital department. Every time I had attended, this was always the case. He has done such a marvellous thing and this will be spread far and wide.

On Tuesday 9th June, at 1pm, Pastor Andrew came over and spent some time with me and my mum in the garden. We gave thanks to the Lord for all He had done through this season. Pastor Andrew said that when he was driving over he had been praying for me and the Holy Spirit gave him the following scripture:-

The bolts of your gates will be
iron and bronze,
and your strength will equal your days.

There is no one like the God
of Jeshurun (Israel)
who rides across the heavens to help you
and on the clouds in his majesty.
The eternal God is your refuge,
and underneath are the everlasting arms.
He will drive out your enemies before you,
saying, 'Destroy them!'
So Israel will live in safety;
Jacob will dwell secure
in a land of grain and new wine,
where the heavens drop dew.
Blessed are you, Israel!
Who is like you,
a people saved by the Lord?
He is your shield and helper
and your glorious sword.

Your enemies will cower before you,
and you will tread on their heights.

(Deuteronomy 33 v 25-29)

We rejoiced as we talked about the similarities between this portion of scripture and some of the content of Psalm 18.

He parted the heavens and came down;
dark clouds were under his feet.
He mounted the cherubim and flew;
he soared on the wings of the wind.
He made darkness his covering, his canopy
around him—
the dark rain clouds of the sky.

(Psalm 18 v 9-11)

Friday 26th June, and it was time for the next virtual review. This time I took the call whilst attempting to navigate my mum through the McDonalds drive thru. We had been for a long walk in the woods and we were passing on the way home.

I was informed that once again, my bloods had returned as excellent and the MRI scan had not highlighted any new areas for concern. It goes without saying that I was questioned as to a possible steroid intake, (this time the pharmacist explained that she had to ask). She was amazed to hear me once again so full of energy and commented that by this stage of treatment, most people cannot tolerate the side effects and quit the treatment. I once again told her that I have experienced no symptom or side effect whatsoever and that it was all glory to God! I was to now to proceed with the next course of treatment.

He shot his arrows and scattered the enemy,
with great bolts of lightning he routed them."

(Psalm 18 v 14)

Friday 24th July, the second to last virtual appointment in this season and once again, I was informed that my bloods had all returned as excellent so time to commence the penultimate course of treatment.

On Friday 28th August, we went out for the day with Steven, my niece and my nephew. Whilst out enjoying our day, I took the last virtual appointment with the hospital on the phone. The lady was once again amazed that I reported no side effects from the previous course of treatment and she commented that very few people make it this far into this stage of treatment. Praise God all bloods had come back excellent once again and so to hit the last course of treatment the following week. I would then receive an appointment to attend for a scan within the following few weeks.

I attended for the MRI scan on 2nd October where I had yet another opportunity to share what God has done for me with a nurse. She was very interested and asked for a copy of this book upon release.

I had a follow up phone call from the consultant the following Tuesday, who said that, although someone else still needed to review the scan, it looked better than the one in June and he could not see any cause for concern. He confirmed there was a lot of scar tissue but I know the Lord will complete the work he has started. I will now enter what the hospital call their *'surveillance system'* where they will invite me for a further scan in three months' time. I will continue to survey the wondrous cross on which Jesus was crucified, taking my sins and all disease upon Himself. He died and rose again so that I could live! Hallelujah! What a Saviour!

While I originally understood that I would be able to apply for my driving licence to be returned ahead of Christmas this year, the consultant now told me that I would not be permitted to drive until 2022. I was disappointed at this news; I was so much looking forward to getting back behind the wheel. However, there will be no limitation whatsoever in me getting to where I need to be for the extension of the Kingdom of God. There are contact details at the end of this book if anyone would like me to share at a church meeting, within a prison, or any other gathering, large or small. The Lord will continue to make a way.

I Hear the Chains Falling

Let the redeemed of the Lord tell their story—
those he redeemed from the hand of the foe.
(Psalm 107 v 2)

Back in January 2020, I had spent a wonderful afternoon with my sister Maggie. Whilst she was knelt at my feet praying, she was hearing clearly from God about some things that were ahead for me and said that the Lord had great things planned for me; plans far beyond anything I could think of or imagine; she later wrote this in a message for me to keep in my testimony book:-

"The Word declared; bodies healed
and lives transformed."

This is all in keeping with the words spoken over me. I am anointed to proclaim the good news of the Kingdom, and release from darkness for the prisoners and the oppressed. This means for those literally sat in prison cells but also for those who are bound in their minds or bodies. I have been trained for war and I believe part of this is for treading on the heights with and for others. The devil has so many of these precious individuals completely bound with no natural way or hope of escape and *lasting* freedom. They may experience a temporary freedom but then relapse or get back in the cycle and re-enter the revolving door. My destiny has been contended for and, likewise, destinies of these individuals are being highly contended for. I will not allow this to happen on my watch when I have been commissioned. The

195

devil does not have the final say over these lives as he has not had over mine. He had attempted to take me out as he knew what release lay ahead for others. Jesus (Jehovah) has had the final say.

The scripture below was prophesied over me by Steven in the early days and, as I write this page in mid June, I testify to this already starting to unfold, the hand of God continually being revealed:-

> *A great door for effective work has opened to*
> *me, and there are many who oppose me.*
> *(1 Corinthians 16 v 9)*

I mentioned in a previous chapter about how the enemy will always fight to the last, firstly, to prevent a child of God realising who they are in Christ and, secondly, to prevent them from entering into the full destiny set out for them by God.

His Boys

I will always remain grateful for the wonderful upbringing I had, but realise this is not something that can be taken for granted. The Father is continuing to break my heart for those things that break his. I have spoken with too many individuals who have walked a path of pain and sorrow and have never had anyone to love them or have ever been told they have done well or that someone is proud of them. I have spoken with many who have never even met their dads or, if they did, have suffered at their hands, resulting in heartbreak and distrust. There are many sons crying for their fathers and many fathers crying like a son. My God is a Father to the Fatherless.

Early in 2020, I sat speechless and wept, whilst watching Gareth Malone work within HMP Aylesbury in putting together a choir. The heart this man had was truly inspirational and confirmed again the heart that the Father has towards these boys; a heart he has given me just a glimpse of.

Jesus told a parable about a shepherd leaving ninety-nine sheep to go looking for the one. Every life is significant and has purpose. I prophesied early on in this journey that there would be Kingdom extension with acceleration on the back of my experience.

> *Then Jesus told them this parable: "Suppose one of you has a hundred sheep and loses one of them. Doesn't he leave the ninety-nine in the open country and go after the lost sheep until he finds it? And when he finds it, he joyfully puts it on his shoulders and goes home. Then he calls his friends and neighbours together and says, 'Rejoice with me; I have found my lost sheep.' I tell you that in the same way there will be more rejoicing in heaven over one sinner who repents than over ninety-nine righteous persons who do not need to repent."*
> *(Luke 15 v 3-7)*

If I can invest in just one prisoner or ex prisoner, and see their life turned around and transformed by the power of Almighty God, all that I have been through will be worth it. However, the God I serve is able to do abundantly *more* than I would even ask or think so I know what lies ahead is huge in terms of impact for the Kingdom. I will continue to tell these boys they are loved, valued and precious.

Just as my chains have come loose *through faith* and I have been healed and set free by the blood of Jesus, many are going to walk out of darkness into the light and realise their potential in Christ, knowing they are loved and fully accepted just as they are, not defined by anything they have done in their past. Chains of shame, addiction, abuse, mental health issues, poverty, brokenness and many others will be smashed off these lives in Jesus Name. These men will become fathers to their children and the cycle will shatter. The excuses that are made to prevent them dealing with the root causes will be exposed and I prophesy this over many lives:-

> *Yet I destroyed the Amorites before them,*
> *though they were tall as the cedars*
> *and strong as the oaks.*
> *I destroyed their fruit above*
> *and their roots below.*
> *(Amos 2:9)*

God has vines to plant for His glory and there is no stately cedar or sturdy oak that he will not uproot in order for this to happen.

> *You transplanted a vine from Egypt;*
> *you drove out the nations and planted it.*
> *You cleared the ground for it,*
> *and it took root and filled the land.*
> *(Psalm 80:8-9)*

It has recently been prophesied that I will be writing another book and that this book will be studded with the testimonies of people that will now shortly be delivered from the hand of the foe, according to Psalm 107. Salvations, healings and miracles; prisoners set free. I call forth the preachers, the evangelists, the pastors from their cells. There are so many with hidden, raw, God-given talents to be invested in the Kingdom.

> *The people living in darkness*
> *have seen a great light;*
> *on those living in the land of the*
> *shadow of death*
> *a light has dawned.*
> *(Matthew 4 v 16)*

Returning to where we started, and the prayer meeting held in our home back on 5th December 2019. The people mentioned in the scripture set out below returned joyfully as do I. The Lord has given me great cause to rejoice over every enemy.

> *Then, led by Jehoshaphat, all the men of*
> *Judah and Jerusalem returned joyfully to*
> *Jerusalem, for the Lord had given them cause*
> *to rejoice over their enemies. They entered*
> *Jerusalem and went to the temple of the Lord*
> *with harps and lyres and trumpets.*
>
> *The fear of God came on all the surrounding*
> *kingdoms when they heard how the Lord had*
> *fought against the enemies of Israel. And the*
> *kingdom of Jehoshaphat was at peace, for his*
> *God had given him rest on every side."*

(2 Chronicles 20 v 27-30)

The hymn my parents chose back in 1978 for my dedication has been walked out and I testify to every line having been true. I have stood on the firm foundation of His Word, cried to Jesus and He has heard and rescued me. I have stood fearless through it all and have received His strength daily. He has called me out upon the water and has caused what should in the natural be deep distress to be used to work towards sanctifying me. He has upheld me all the way through.

'For my thoughts are not your thoughts,
neither are your ways my ways,'
declares the Lord.
'As the heavens are higher than the earth,
so are my ways higher than your ways
and my thoughts than your thoughts.
As the rain and the snow
come down from heaven,
and do not return to it
without watering the earth
and making it bud and flourish,
so that it yields seed for the sower and bread for
the eater,
so is my word that goes out from my mouth:
it will not return to me empty,
but will accomplish what I desire
and achieve the purpose for which I sent it.
You will go out in joy
and be led forth in peace;
the mountains and hills
will burst into song before you,

***and all the trees of the field
will clap their hands.***

(Isaiah 55 v 8-12)

His amazing grace has been sufficient as I have walked through the fire and there has been a refining. All hell may have sought to shake me but He remained true to His Word and has not forsaken me. I have felt His presence continually with me and have never had such a close walk with Him in all the years I have known Him.

Graduation Day

On week six of the Sycamore Tree course at HMP Winchester, all participants are encouraged to prepare and present an act of restitution. This can be a poem, song, painting, letter or similar – whatever it is, it is always special. A lot of work and determination is put in to these works of art and when the boys make the very brave step to stand at the front, they are encouraged all the way. These efforts are outstanding and quite often bring a tear to the eye of everyone on the team. Some of these boys really struggle to receive praise, but these are moments we are very proud of.

I thought I would take a turn myself and sum up my recent experience.

~

A is for ***anointing*** breaking the yoke, all ***authority*** been given to the King on the throne; the ***ark*** may have rocked from side to side, but not one drop of water got inside; I'm on ***assignment*** now and wow, what a trip, but hallelujah, the enemy lost his filthy grip; daughter ***Anna*** has been ***awesome*** throughout, our crying with laughter, never without; Pastor ***Andrew***, in less than the hour, you were on the case against the devourer.

B is for ***battlefield*** where the warriors stood, the ***blood*** stained ***banner*** held up as it should; on and off the field, taking their turns, not counting the cost, just using their shields; daughter ***Beth***, you have been great, now seventeen as I sit and relate; a race for our licence shortly begins, try pass your test before Christmas Eve; **blessings** and **boys** with their lives turned around, one of the fruits of enduring this now; **Beki**, my sister, from the waters I rise, many coming with me, time for new life; my fellow **blonde Bethan**, just one thing, don't admit to falling over when my line you ring; a **book** was to be written, two prophetic words given, the Holy Spirit and I had already connected and on Him I relied, I started to write as prompted and got the story down, every chapter running over and with His Word aligned, a second book is underway, many will be writing, having come into the way, littered with testimonies as I bring in the sheaves, rejoicing and celebration, still more to retrieve.

C is for 2 **Chronicles** 20 and the **cross** of Jesus **Christ**, every **curse** broken, **chain** loosed, **confrontation**, a waste of enemy time; **Catherine**, our afternoons together have been so rich, encounters with the Holy Spirit never to be missed; we saw the seasons change, move on, knowing that the battle was won and now we wait for you to minister behind the walls and see the opening of many doors.

D is for **declarations**, simply speaking out the truth, **divine** life is my portion, I'm the living proof; **dancing** and rejoicing has always been the theme, although never the expectation or plan of the enemy; little nephew **David,** your Grandad would be proud and would love to have come and joined us every time when you were round; Pastor **Dennis**, a General in the faith, we will soon rejoice on your platform and have the room erupt in praise; you failed to board an aircraft in obedience to the Lord and walked beside me through the valley, victory assured; you shut yourself in closets and gathered a band of men, to do battle through appointments, no matter what the land, Israel, Norway or home in the UK, you always found the time to cry out and pray; intercessory prayer was what was needed and your story of this having preceded; a **Deborah** in the making has been the prophetic word, this season never been in vain, there are those who have not yet heard.

E is for **exposure** of the **enemy's** lies, time for **exploits** now, it's the season to arise; upon **eagles** wings is where I have soared, rising high above the storm; **energy** boundless and a song of praise, always more than sufficient to get through each day.

F is for **fearless**, I took a stand, realising this battle was not being fought by a man; walking by **faith**, the sense of sight never the plan, without this it remains impossible to please God, pleasing only man; my sister **Faith**, what can I say, all those times you have stopped to pray, The Spirit of God is on the move and we remain standing in the way; **failed** enemy assignment, he thought he had won but all that resulted was more light being shone; **foul** play trying to take me out at the wheel, we already heard about you going for the heel; however, we stand triumphant as I point you to the cross, here my Jesus shed His blood and your dirty head was crushed.

G is for **glory** and the **goodness** of **God**, chasing me down whilst a **giant** is withstood; my sister **Grace**, this you saw and after three times, he fell to the floor; *Gands*, there is no doubt at all, selected for me by *God*, your department met with radiance and consequently His love; only He could ordain prayer meetings with me praying for your staff, hair you tied in bunches despite later working with only half.

H is for *healing* and *HMPS*, the mission continues with the best days ahead; *honoured* I stand with the Governor Deputy, writing for me my foreword as we march to victory; He made my feet like *hinds* feet and stood me on my *heights*, running up and down the rocks and enabling me to climb; Father I ask that you keep breaking my *heart* for all the things that break yours, I have not journeyed along this road for nothing, I know there is more.

I is for *intimacy* and this with Christ; *'It is well'*, the words declared, every time I arise; I thank you so much Jesus for healing me, in accordance with Your Word found in Psalm 103.

J is for *joy* and what a fountain there has been, inexpressible, contagious and full of glory; sister *Juanita* and your team of praying mums, I thank you all for the time you gave and the battle you have done; Pastor *Julia,* a whole chapter you wrote, you have been so faithful while I remained in the boat, we have stood firm on the Word for no side effects, only speaking life, we stood, He did the rest; *Josh,* despite some of the things we have walked through during the last four years, mercy has *always* triumphed as we have changed up and down gears, there have been many a high and many a low but God has been faithful, despite not understanding our loads, it has been an honour and privilege to stand by you, north or south of the country, I have sought to remain true.

K is for **_Kingdom_** and the return of my **_keys_**; yet another failed attempt at stopping the mission, there is no stopping me; **_Kiran_**, your word confirmed this, there is healing for the sick, despite the enemy trying to deter, these hands are blessed for this; **_Karen_** whilst in Eastbourne, back in 2015, you saw a vision whilst praying with me, I was wielding a sword and holding a huge shield, little did we know what was to later be revealed; **_Kelly_** and the team, I so appreciate you, supporting our young people is what we do; upon my return the love I felt, a regular to panel, never in doubt.

L is for **_lifts_** and these purely for mission, as even the treatment was permitted for Kingdom extension; time in the prison was never at stake, the enemy is a **_liar_** and can't keep the gate; my brother **_Lloyd_**, we have had a **_laugh_** , sometimes it was a struggle for you to get your words out, through initial treatments, you checked in every day, whether up the scaffold, at work or at play, you prayed for my sleep and this every night, even if late and I turned out the light; sister in law **_Lottie_**, I still wait for your shop, Poundland supplies I remain without, you had best hope they remain in stock, a normal visit for me, remember I grab the lot; **_Laurel_**, my sister, the songs you have sent have always been full of truth and not sentiment, with you there is no messing, this is so refreshing, and out of this season, our being sisters, remaining a blessing; sister **_Lucille,_** whilst praying one day, you saw an angel warrior standing beside me, guarding my way, with feet slightly parted and folded arms, he was huge; "*Just you try it mate*", the words that he used; *Lynne*, I have got to know you in a new way, your faithful commitment to praying at the start of the day, you set an alarm to wake with me, to pray and seek the Lord through to complete victory.

M is for *mother* heart, always wanting to reach out, despite this leading to heartbreak and one trip down a path, this had not put me off as grace abounds more, lies all forgiven, and so I love more; pressing on, I will walk wherever He leads, to the boys sat in darkness or fallen to their knees, prison doors swinging open and the result being free, to the fatherless, addicts, homeless, a Father He will be. My *mum* known as *Mother*, *Muriel*, Grape or Jan, you have been all that you have needed to be, always knowing the plan, when I first stepped into the department, you knew I did not belong, this was never my portion, the journey had simply begun.

N is for '*null* and void', '*not* known at this address', the enemy faced with the Blood, his weapons defective, dropped as he fled; *Niece Naomi* and the sign outside, I only got this sorted just in time, she tried gaining entry but this was a challenge as Auntie Fi has locked her out, *Nanny* now waiting with her baggage, visits to play centres always a theme, a trip with uncle Peter arranged with glee.

O is for *opportunities* that lie ahead, lots of travelling the country, the news of Jesus being spread; *Outlook* will be busy as bookings roll on in; **Obadiah** 17 is the place it all begins; **Olly** and your crew, so grateful for you, the streets of Hounslow burning bright as you do what you do, your voice notes received, so timely, bang on, your big day I now await to celebrate with you; my steps have been **ordered** and these by the Spirit, from that day in November right through, there's no limit.

P is for **prayer** and without a doubt, **prison**, the place established for my primary mission; **Psalm** 18, my story for sure, devil you see what happened when you tried knocking my door, I am possessing my possessions and moving in new ways, plundering your kingdom will take many days; my patient husband, my perfect match **Pete**, I guess the most challenging season we yet had to meet, I thank you so much for loving me throughout, serving and running as always no doubt; **Palm** Sunday was the Sunday that I was born, a day around the time we remember the thorns, a triumphant procession, a joyous parade, when the city you entered, a way was made, branches thrown down, make way for the king, honour was to follow, what a selfless offering.

Q is for **question**, so what comes next? I have never asked why, proof written in text; I have no money for what my heart longs to do, but this does not matter as that step I followed through, He told me for sure we were crossing aside, me knowing for certain, He would provide; throughout He has done this and He ain't stopping now, as I continue stepping out and pressing on for my crown; what is round the corner is not for me to know, the **quest** for souls is where I am to go; wherever this leads me and whatever the cost, this will always result in reaching the lost; this is His plan and this is His heart, He has always seen me willing stood right at the start; I have gone through the fire and come out refined, although not perfect, I press on for the prize.

R is for '*return* to sender' as I prepare for work; the Lord's *Report* being all that matters, the rest just simply murk; *Reverend Rosemary* Taylor, you have been so good, always there encouraging me, *rallying* the troops, you called me from Barbados Christmas 2019, you have sent me songs, stood so firm and helped rout the enemy; my sister *Rita*, times got sweeter, as with *Raphael* and Vera you stood, despite not living nearer, our friendship has become dearer and it was obvious it would; *Rachel* and Nev, I long for the day when myself and Pete can come over your way, the invite for brunch, dinner or lunch to sit in your garden and stay; sat long in the sun, discussing the fun of all that is ahead, a new day.

S is for *salvation*, come and *survey, sin*, death and *sickness* all put away; my brother *Steven*, you have been so good, rock solid, on fire and grounded in Truth; *Shir*, your poor time keeping never fails to amaze, sometimes leaving me waiting for days, however, New Year's Eve, a surprise you gave, as upon entering the road to park, you were seen heading the other way, unbelievably, at last you did it, an hour and a half til midnight, you take it to the limit. *Sue,* at the start, when you first heard the news, 'through' was the word the Spirit laid upon you, simply walking in, through and out, my shepherd with me without a shadow of a doubt.

T is for *troop* that I have advanced, in the natural impossible, not even a chance but because of you, this I could do and *triumphant* I stand having taken the land; *trampled* and *trembling* underfoot, the enemy's neck firm under my foot, "you ain't going nowhere" whilst I stand and declare, God is so good and for you, I don't care.

U is for '*undeliverable*', and not received, the Word of God is clear, the condition was not for me; you sought to confront me, and that you did, however, I had backup and once again you slid; you slithery snake, not long now and you'll be heading to the lake where you will remain in hell, every battle He has won and you will never overcome; the one who fought for me has won the victory, this is now and forever the cry of my heart, I was born a winner right from the start, with Christ inside of me, how can I lose? He is my living hope and this He has proved; peace has been my *umpire* the whole way through, a peace transcending *understanding*, so many confused; the *Upper* Room prayer meeting where the homeless slept downstairs, was a time to be remembered as we waited and we shared, the fire of the Holy Spirit fell afresh that night and the fullness of His power with resurrection life.

V is for *victory*, this having been won, the very same day the Father rose His Son, we have simply been standing on the Word of the Lord, enforcing what Jesus has already done; *Victor*, my brother, a man of faith, you have stood with me from the middle to the end of the race, from the sidelines cheered, "keep upping the gear", the end is in sight and enemy to flight.

W is for *warrior*, she leapt over the walls, verse 29 of Psalm 18, read here, this records, strength has been renewed daily whilst I have *waited* on the Lord, this in line with Pastor Ron's *word*, he shared prior to 24th.

X is for 'ex' offenders (well, I did my best!), the next book will tell you more, many testimonies, first hand to be shared.

Y is for my *young* person, my hero, you pulled me from my car, to your boyfriend's we were heading, it wasn't very far, without warning, that Thursday morning, things turned around, one moment sat at the wheel, the next unconscious on the ground, today and forever, we both wear a scar, the one on my head, will be heard near and far, it speaks of His love and tells of His grace, I am left with no choice but to give Him the praise, I pray now all trauma break off of your life, and a new season you enter, far away from strife.

Z is for *zeal* for the work of the Lord, the great commission walked out as I yield to the call, to lead His boys home, is part of this story and the result of this, the manifestation of His glory, as these men return one by one, chains being loosed and shackles gone, snatched from the grip of the enemy, royal robes put around them and a surge of energy, the arms of the Father ready to embrace, come on now boys, it's time to run the race; people often comment that my face turns aglow, as I share the heart He has given me, I am now trained to bend a bow.

My Weapon is a Melody

I have worshipped, praised and sang my way through this journey and my family will testify to this (I am always singing praises). The day I first got back on my feet back in December I was up praising and rejoicing. I now look forward to the day when all that have stood with me meet together to rejoice and celebrate.

Pastor Julia writes:-

"I was both surprised and honoured to be asked to write something for this wonderful book... where do I start?

On a Sunday morning at Victory Gospel Church back in December 2019, we were preparing for church when Pastor Andrew, our senior pastor, advised the pastoral team that Fi would be coming for prayer...at the end of November, she had been pulled from her car following a seizure, and a brain tumour had been diagnosed. To be honest I could not think who Fi was, but as soon as this 'petite blonde bombshell' bounced through the doors I remembered her immediately. She arrived with her mum, she looked RADIANT... full of smiles, full of energy and the Zeal of the Lord...Full of Faith. I didn't know at this time, but the week before she had undergone brain surgery and the staples were still in her head!

On Christmas Eve, the staples were removed but the diagnosis from the doctors was poor. "The most aggressive form of brain tumour, a sort that apparently likes to 'invade'" (This is a quote from Fi's own messenger reports – I have kept every communication as a witness and a testimony to this woman's faith and the faithfulness of our God), an intense course of radiotherapy, chemo, a mammogram and a gastroscopy were to follow very quickly. Fi's response (again her own words) "The appointment has not moved me at all. Psalm 18 all the way"

I knew from this we were not ministering to someone who had conceded to the idea of an early death, but to someone who had faith in what Jesus' death on the cross, and His resurrection had bought for her... A divine exchange – HE DIED so she would LIVE.

Fi wanted us to stand with her in agreement... agreeing with her faith filled words and with the Word of God...Trusting God for the breakthrough.

Jesus says "If two of you agree on earth concerning anything that they ask, It will be done for them by my Father in heaven" (Matthew 18:19)

I was reminded of a scripture in Exodus 17: 8-16. The enemy had come to steal the water (represents life). Some were chosen to aid in the battle (those standing shoulder to shoulder with Fi, in prayer and encouragement)

But Moses hands became heavy so they took a stone and put it under him and he sat on it.

214

And Aaron and Hur supported his hands on one side and the other side" This I feel has been part of my role along with many others...to enable her, like Moses, to hold her ground on the top of the hill with the word of God held forth like a banner.

(Exodus 17 v12)

I want to share with you some of the many FAITH CONFESSIONS and PRAISE REPORTS Fi has made during this time (again direct quotes from her messages)

30th December 2019... "Hey! Get ready to praise!!...Glory to the Lamb... mammogram completely clear and no need for ultrasound...Hallelujah."

3rd January 2020... the day before attending gastroscopy. "Even though I walk THROUGH the valley, Hallelujah, my cup overflows. Later - NO FURTHER ACTION REQUIRED!"

9th January 2020... "I nullify every single effect of any treatments in Jesus name"

15th January 2020... Inspired by the song "I raise a hallelujah in the presence of my enemies", Fi starts next prison course for 20 new boys.

16th   January 2020... treatment planning meeting. "I am believing for NO ill effects from treatment in Jesus' name... I am continuing to stand strong in My GOD who is able to do far above anything I could even imagine or ask for...I am so excited about sharing my testimony for the Glory of the King"

17th January 2020..."By Faith NO SIDE EFFECTS... all bloods normal... and the Glory of God will be seen all over me."

Throughout treatment it has been exactly as she has stated in faith. Fi has walked in favour and blessing and has continued to "Shine for His glory". Each week she has bounced into church full of life, joy, peace and Faith.

10th February 2020..."The God I serve knows only how to triumph! What an awesome day this has been!"

17th February 2020..."This Gospel WILL NOT KNEEL and SHALL NOT FAINT". "I am pursuing, overtaking and recovering ALL in Jesus name"

31st March 2020 in the face of a negative report...Fi continues to shine forth the glory

My final quote (just a few of so many) from Fi... Resurrection Sunday 12th April 2020...The world is in lockdown due to COVID-19 Virus and Fi has completed a week of double dose treatments that she was told would leave her exhausted and debilitated...she defies the negative report with faith "I am dancing about I tell you! I have a river of life and joy"

"I am looking forward to the biggest testimony and praise party[3] … we will dust off our dancing shoes and give praise and glory to our faithful God"

Pastor Julia Franklin (13th April 2020)

---

[3] Due to the pandemic, the praise party has to be postponed until restrictions are fully lifted.

Fi's Mum Writes

"I thank and praise the Lord so much for the peace and joy Fi has known since the very beginning of this season which she is passing through. Also, for her unwavering faith in Jesus her Saviour and healer as she continues to stand on the unchanging promises of God and The Living Word.

Visits to hospital had their lighter moments as we share a similar sense of humour and usually found something to laugh about (on more than one occasion, we have been crying with laughter!) More importantly were the times Fi had the opportunity to share and pray for staff in the treatment room when they asked her to.

We have enjoyed our long daily walks together during lockdown, social distancing never being a problem, Fi always having been a fast walker, was always way ahead of me, even on days she was having treatment. We have sometimes seen an elderly man tending his garden and he always greets Fi with "Hello smiley lady".

It is amazing how the Lord has kept Fi through both radio and chemotherapy, alongside other medications. Even when the dose of chemo was doubled and then increased further, she experienced no side effects. The only thing that has happened is she has lost some of her hair due to the intense radiotherapy.

I thank the Lord for a very good and supportive son-in-law, wonderful husband and father and I am blessed to have his help when needed. During lockdown, Pete has delivered 'meals on wheels' on a Sunday which has been very much appreciated.

Every day we have seen new mercies and blessings, prayers answered, a word given and then confirmed speaking right into a given situation just at the right moment; very uplifting and encouraging.

I Praise God for His mighty army of people who have been there right from the start, for their faithful prayer, support, love and time given and so much more. I thank the Lord so much for all of you."

With Grateful Thanks

I start by honouring and thanking my wonderful husband of nineteen years; for standing by me, praying for me and loving me unconditionally throughout. I thank you for encouraging me and being proud of me back in the hospital when I could not move my arm but kept trying and did not give up. We have travelled the same valley albeit along very different paths. However, there has been abundant daily grace for every need and we will come out together, stronger and united. I am excited about all that lies ahead for us as a family and I love you with all my heart.

Beth, you have been truly amazing. At what has been a time of major transition in your life, you have remained rock solid and displayed attributes of someone a lot older.

Anna, again, you have been awesome. We have shared many a tear of laughter and will never stop. So many funny memories...

Grandad would be so proud of us all; again, the fruit of his prayers. Like two warriors, you have both stood immovable throughout and your faith is strong. You know the God we love and serve and He has never and will never fail us.

**Blessed are those who fear the Lord,
who find great delight in his commands.**

Their children will be mighty in the land;
the generation of the upright will be blessed.
(Psalm 112 v 1-2)

My mum; I can't thank you enough for all you have been to me through this season. You have always been at the end of the phone and outside of lockdown, over every day, doing all you could to ease the load, especially allowing Pete to get to work by becoming my taxi to the shops, prison, church and hospital. Many a laugh we have had along the way. I thank you for having set your alarm to get up to pray through weeks of treatment. Thank you also for your written contribution.

Steven, I struggle to put this down as words cannot express my gratitude for all you have been to me this last season, an absolute legend. You have filled the place of honour that we both know our dad would have taken and you have done us both proud; you took the baton from him and ran hard with it; you are definitely up there with my best friends and I so appreciate our shared sense of humour. How many times through this do you reckon we have cried with laughter together in person and over the phone? Thank you so much for your written contribution.

Lottie; thank you for passing on updates for prayer and praise reports and also for arranging for your ladies bible study group to pray. I have enjoyed the times you have been down as a family, always been good sat round with your two little 'miracles', Naomi and David; love them lots and they never fail to bring a smile.

Special thanks to everyone listed in the following section for standing in the gap for me, I cannot express how grateful I am for all the love and prayer support I have received:-

All at Victory Gospel Church (Southampton), Kings Community Church (Southampton), River of Life Church (Southampton), Pastor Joseph and Kristos Church (Kenya), Good Shepherd Gospel Church (Southampton), Hope Church (West Wickham), Sholing Elim Church (Southampton), Christchurch (Winchester), Worldwide Mission Fellowship (London), Pastor Dennis Greenidge, Pastor Rosemary Taylor, Pastor Andrew White & wife Jo, Pastors Ron & Margaret (Pastor Ron, thank you for your written contribution), Pastor Josh & wife Aby, Pastors Julia & Paul (Pastor Julia, thank you for your written contribution), Pastors Jim & Wen, Pastors Richard & Tina, Pastor Toni, Reverend Margaret Hague, Grace, Maggie, Laurel, Lloyd (thank you for your written contribution), Charles & Pamela, Vivienne & Alice, Lucille, Mavis & Roy, Ace & Susana, Juanita & your team of praying mums, Victor & Vivien, Kiran, Ashaki, Vergi & Matthew, Rebekah & Daryl (Rebekah, thank you for your written contribution), Catherine (thank you for your written contribution), Bethan (thank you for your written contribution), Beki & Steve, Steph, Andy & Janet, Chris & Charlotte, Nick, Tim, Martin, Martyn, Josh T, Faith & Pete, Elaine & Ian, Shir, Sue B, Gandhi aka Gands, Sherwin & Evelyn, Alex & Alethia, Marilyn & Phil, Rita, Raphael, Vera, Peter & Veronica, Tim & Carolyn, John & Judy, Lynne,

Pauline, Sue, Rachel & Nev, Jacqui, Mike, Rod, Jane, all Prison Fellowship prayer group members across the region, some who wish to remain unnamed, Ray & Vi (Vi, thank you for your written contribution), Olly Sherwood aka King Jims & your group 'Men of Honour', (Olly, thank you for your written contribution), Dave & Megan (Dave, thank you for your written contribution), Darren, Karen & Karl, Alasdair & Hilary, Jan.

Josh, thank you for your written contribution. You gave me the honour of being godmother to your beautiful boy; thank you. I will always treasure our cuddles, in particular the one where he fell asleep for an hour in my arms; now safely in the arms of Jesus.

Karl & Gillian, thank you for collecting my car and returning it home for us on that Saturday in November.

Sean, my 'bodyguard', you walked me to the anaesthetic room and gave me your hand to hold, thank you.

Yvonne, you saved the day and sorted my hair; thank you.

Shane, you visited and shared your testimony within HMP Winchester alongside your beautiful wife Sam; thank you.

Special thanks also to all at HMP Winchester, in particular Deputy Governor, Susie Richardson. Thank you for finding time in your busy schedule to write the foreword. I look forward to continuing to serve together alongside you within and without the walls. You have also managed to arrange for an inmate to design the front cover for my book from my outline description. Thank you so much Karl. Thank you also to Senior Chaplain David Hinks, Reverend Cliff McClelland (thank you for your written contribution) and the rest of the Chaplaincy Team, thank you for hosting Sycamore Tree; I would also like to thank all the staff across the establishment; myself and my team so appreciate all that you do.

Thank you to all at Step by Step for covering my absence and for all your love and support upon my return to work back in April. Thank you too, to my hero of a young person; you helped to save my life. Thank you also to whoever assisted you that day whilst you waited for the emergency services to arrive. I will most likely never know who you were but I am so grateful for you stopping and taking the time.

Thank you to all at Southampton General Hospital, through all the departments I have visited; I appreciate all that you have done in your professional capacity in caring for me. Everyone I have had dealings with has been amazing. Many of you have been curious as to how I have been keeping so well and have no answer... I hope this book helps to answer some of your questions.

I end by thanking Kerry, the nurse at the local surgery who has been taking my bloods through lockdown.

With This I Close

Consider it pure joy, my brothers and sisters, whenever you face trials of many kinds, because you know that the testing of your faith produces perseverance. Let perseverance finish its work so that you may be mature and complete, not lacking anything.
(James 1 v 2-4)

I hope that you have enjoyed reading; my second book is under way.

If you would like to get in contact, please email me at: **thefinalsay@outlook.com**

Printed in Great Britain
by Amazon